The MEDICARE SURVIVAL GUIDE

2015 EDITION

DIANE DANIELS

authorHOUSE®

AuthorHouse™
1663 Liberty Drive
Bloomington, IN 47403
www.authorhouse.com
Phone: 1 (800) 839-8640

© 2015 Diane Daniels. All rights reserved.

No part of this book may be reproduced, stored in a retrieval system, or transmitted by any means without the written permission of the author.

Published by AuthorHouse   04/30/2015

ISBN: 978-1-5049-0526-8 (sc)
ISBN: 978-1-5049-0527-5 (e)

Library of Congress Control Number: 2015905246

Written by – Diane Daniels
Cover design – iQ Branding
Edited by – Norma Jean Lutz

Print information available on the last page.

Any people depicted in stock imagery provided by Thinkstock are models, and such images are being used for illustrative purposes only. Certain stock imagery © Thinkstock.

This book is printed on acid-free paper.

Because of the dynamic nature of the Internet, any web addresses or links contained in this book may have changed since publication and may no longer be valid. The views expressed in this work are solely those of the author and do not necessarily reflect the views of the publisher, and the publisher hereby disclaims any responsibility for them.

The author and publisher disclaim any responsibility for any liability, loss, or risk, personal or otherwise, which is incurred as a consequence, directly or indirectly, from the use and application of any of the content of this book.

Table of Contents

Why I'm Passionate about Medicare............................... vii
Introduction..xv
Chapter 1   The History of Medicare............................. 1
Chapter 2   Do You Know Your A, B, C and Ds? 8
Chapter 3   Types of Medicare Plans 47
Chapter 4   Special Election Periods (SEP) 63
Chapter 5   Turning 65... 69
Chapter 6   End Stage Renal Disease (ESRD) 73
Chapter 7   Veterans... 87
Chapter 8   Medicare Transsexual Surgery 95
Conclusion.. 99
References Cited...101
About the Author 103

WHY I'M PASSIONATE ABOUT MEDICARE

There are people you meet in your life and you know you'll never forget them. It may be family members, or it may be a friend, or it could be a total stranger. Nanny, my great-grandmother, was that person for me. She has had the greatest impact on my life – no one else has even come close.

Running a close second was my maternal grandmother who also was a deciding factor in my life for the highest good.

People often ask me why I'm so passionate about Medicare, and these two women are part of the reason why. Let me explain.

Just Be a Kid

When you're ten years old, you don't care about money, politics, or wars. Kids shouldn't have to worry about those kinds of things. You're a kid and you should be able to live your life as a kid. Thanks to my mom, she made sure I had every opportunity to do just that – be a kid.

My parents were getting divorced. All I knew was that my sisters and I were going to be living with my father at my paternal grandmother's house. After that, we only saw my mom on weekends.

It was very difficult to get acclimated to a different house, living with your grandmother, grandfather, your aunt and your father all at the same time. My sisters and I were sent to public school for the first time. I had been in Catholic school my entire life – all ten years of it – kindergarten up to fourth grade in Catholic school. I was used to nuns, prayers, and discipline. I had no idea what the school world was like without them. But I soon found out.

Public School

The public school was located across the street from my grandparent's house. The huge playground was the view out my grandparent's front window. We walked to school. We wore regular clothes to school. It was familiar wearing my white button blouse, brown and white saddle shoes and a plaid jumper to school. At first, it was cool to wear regular clothes and sneakers to school, but it got old quick. I only had a few outfits I liked and I soon found myself wishing I had that stupid uniform back. *Geez!* What was wrong with me?

In class, after an assignment, we could do pretty much what we wanted. Read a book, read an SRA booklet, play a game. Play a game? I wasn't use to that. I was used to finishing my work and either starting more work, or sitting on my hands until the rest of the class was done. I didn't know what to do with *freedom*.

My grandparents were loving and kind. My dad and his family tried to make our stay as comfortable as possible. I loved them all very much. It just wasn't the same as being home with my mom and to be able to see Nanny and Grandma (my maternal grandmother) every day. That is what I was comfortable with.

Returning Home

After several months of telling mom we wanted to come back home, we finally did. One Sunday, my dad told me mom was coming to pick us up and take us home. He told us we'd see him on weekends and we would now be living with mom. We got in the car and headed back to Brooklyn!

Next thing I knew, we were moving in with Nanny and Grandma. That was the most awesome thing that could have happened to me and my sisters. If I could have lived with Nanny for the rest of my life, I would have. I loved her that much.

We moved into the basement apartment. In my grandmother's neighborhood they had row houses – like townhouses – all lined up and down one street. Each house had a stoop with its own upper entrance and a separate lower basement entrance. From inside the basement apartment there were stairs that led to the upper apartment with a door that separated the two living quarters. You could lock the door for privacy when you wanted it and opened the door to run in and out of the two apartments.

The basement apartment had one huge living room. The living room and bedroom were combined. I had a twin bed along with my sister who is two years younger than me. My younger sister slept with my mom. The apartment had a separate kitchen and bathroom. It was a pretty good setup.

My mom worked long hours and during the school year I only saw her briefly in the morning and then on weekends.

Diane Daniels

It was pretty tough on her. Like I said, my mom made sure we had a roof over our heads, food to eat, went to school, and most important, we were able to live our lives as kids!

Thank you mom for that. I love you very much for sacrificing so much in your life for me.

The Best Years

The best years of my life were between ten and thirteen years old. I went to school during the day and played outside all afternoon until dinner time. During the summer, I was never inside. I played from morning till it was dark and we couldn't see the ball anymore. Being able to be a kid was the best medicine for me while being in the middle of a divorce.

Nanny was around 85 years old when I was 10. Nanny always told us she didn't know what year she was born. I knew her birthday was May 31, but I never knew the year. My mom didn't know; my grandmother didn't know. It didn't matter because Nanny was perfect just the way she was. I didn't care how old she was. At 85, she was making us lunch, sometimes dinner, and she was loving us to death.

My grandmother worked too. She was the secretary for a shipping company, and worked Monday through Friday from nine-to-five. She took the Flatbush Avenue bus every day, rain or shine.

Awesome Summer

Summers were awesome. I woke up, had breakfast, got in a few cartoons, and watched the clock till it was nine o'clock. Then I was out the door. Usually one or two of my friends were already in the alley throwing a ball around. If no one was out yet, I just went over to their house and called on them to come out.

At lunchtime Nanny yelled my name from the back porch, "Di-ane, Di-ane."

When I approached, Nanny was holding my lunch in her hand. She knew I would come running in the back gate, grab the sandwich and run back out to play. Nanny was awesome like that. She never forced me to sit inside for lunch. She was just happy that I was eating; she never wanted to rob me from having fun.

By five-thirty, supper was on the table. No excuses. When Nanny called at that time, I knew I had to get in gear and get home. I could get away with being called twice, but on the third call I would be grounded.

At that time of evening, you could hear all the kids being called home. "John-ny!" "Te-rry!" "Ka-thy!" No one wanted to leave in the middle of a game. We cut it short by calling out the score, the outs, and who was up, and agreed on everything before we headed inside.

From six to seven the news came on. ABC news to be exact. We always watched the news. But I was waiting for the Good Humor man. He came around seven on summer evenings. I'd wait to hear the bells ringing. As soon as I heard them, I'd yell out, "Who wants ice cream?" Everyone did. Grandma handed over a few dollars and me and my sister were out the door.

Ice cream time was about the time Mom arrived home. She was too exhausted to entertain three kids. We lay on our beds and watched TV till bedtime.

The next day was the same. And so was the next. That's a good thing. Kids need routine. Kids do well with routine

Diane Daniels

Nanny's Stories

I loved hearing Nanny's stories of when she was a little girl in Ireland. She lived on a farm which was very different from growing up in Brooklyn.

One story I particularly liked, was when she was sent to pick up groceries. She rode a donkey with two baskets strapped across its back in which to put the groceries. The trip took more than an hour to get to the little grocery store. On one occasion, Nanny had purchased groceries and distributed them in the two baskets.

As she was riding home, Nanny got distracted and was late returning home. A fierce rainstorm had come up. By the time Nanny reached the creek, it was overflowing. She had to cross the creek to get home.

She led the donkey into the creek, but the water level was so high it reached the baskets on the donkey's back. All the groceries were getting soaked. Nanny pulled the donkey across the creek in chest-high waters. When Nanny finally arrived home, most of the groceries were ruined.

Nanny said her mother ran out to meet her and instead of yelling at her for being late and ruining the groceries, Nanny's mom hugged her and kissed her and kept asking her if she was all right.

I loved that story, because it demonstrated to me how much her mother loved her. Nanny was late and the food was ruined, yet all her mother cared about was her! No wonder our Nanny was always so positive, so loving, and so supportive.

Learning Respect

Nanny and my grandmother taught me to respect authority and to respect my elders. One day I broke a neighbor's window when I was playing stickball. After I ran home so as not to get caught, my grandmother asked me, "What's wrong Diane?"

"Nothing, Grandma."

She knew better. "What's wrong, honey? Whatever it is, as long as you tell me the truth, we'll work it out. If you lie, you'll suffer the consequences."

So I told my grandmother about the broken window. She grabbed her purse and asked me to show her where the neighbor lived. We walked to the house where a man answered Grandma's knock on the door.

"My granddaughter tells me she accidently broke your window while playing ball with the children."

The man said, "So you're the one who broke the window and ran away."

"Diane came home to tell me that she broke the window," Grandma explained to him. "I'm here to pay for the cost to repair it."

The man brought us inside and Grandma wrote a check for the broken window. We left and went home. Grandma never said another word about the incident. And neither did I.

Not every situation went as smoothly as that one, but I learned that nothing good comes out of lying. It's a great lesson for a kid to learn. Till this day, I hold the truth as the utmost in character. I've told my niece and nephews that story as well as other children.

Diane Daniels

Being Around Older Adults

For much of my life, I've been around older adults and I've always respected them. I felt safe and I knew if I needed to know anything I could always ask.

When I was in fifth grade, a girl in my class was always hungry. When I was getting ready to go home for lunch each day, this girl would ask me what I was having.

With Nanny it was definitely pot luck. This young girl then asked me to bring her something to eat. I asked her why she wasn't eating lunch. And she said, "My mom can't buy me lunch tickets."

When I told Nanny the story, she sent me back to school with a sandwich for the girl every day after. In about two weeks' time, the girl wasn't in school anymore. But for those few days, I knew it made a difference in her life.

I learned that helping someone who is less fortunate can make a big impact – no matter how small the gesture. To this day, helping others is part of my daily life.

The Opportunity to Pay Back

I can never thank Nanny and Grandma enough for what they did for me during that difficult time in my childhood. They gave me everything I needed; they set the foundation for my adult life.

Which brings me back to the subject of this book. By educating people about Medicare, I truly feel that in a small way I am paying back these two very special *senior citizen* ladies. It's much more than just a simple "Thank you." Because every time I educate someone about Medicare, I always think about these two lovely women, who forever impacted my life.

INTRODUCTION

You're turning 65 and stereotyped as ready to retire. You are most likely eligible for the government health insurance program called Medicare. You're entering the *golden years* of your life. So why do you feel so lousy?

Perhaps you feel lousy because first of all you're not ready to retire. You like where you're working right now – or maybe you'd like to do something you always loved such as getting into photography, or building handcrafted furniture, or becoming more active in civic affairs.

No need to let an age number rule your life! Many of my clients recently turned 65 and some of them are having the time of their lives. You can be that person!

A Good Thing

Being eligible for Medicare is a good thing! You've paid high health insurance premiums for a long time. You've paid into payroll taxes your entire working life. Enroll in the Medicare program and let the U.S. government pay for 80% of your health care.

What's that? You don't know HOW to enroll in Medicare? But you've known about Medicare your whole working life. You've been paying a payroll tax to help fund the program. Politicians talk about Medicare all the time. You see the private health insurance companies – who are contracted by Medicare – on all the TV commercials. Sunday papers come complete with colorful inserts telling all about Medicare information. Information about Medicare is everywhere!

You Don't Have a Clue

Maybe this is the second reason you feel lousy! You still don't have a clue exactly *how* to enroll in Medicare. You don't really understand Medicare because information about Medicare is so *confusing* and *overwhelming,* and yet *education* for Medicare is sorely lacking.

The government has had to *down-size*, which means employees may be doing the work of two or three people for the same pay and in the same number of hours. This results in a lack of quality.

Not User Friendly

What is the government's standard answer to most Medicare questions? Go to the Medicare.gov website. The problem with that answer is the Medicare.gov website is *not* user friendly.

I'm on that website almost every day and I can tell you that even I find it to be extremely frustrating. Depending on your computer experience and knowledge of Medicare, you would need to spend at least four to eight hours on the website just to get a basic understanding of what Medicare is all about.

Who has that kind of time?

Not you. You should be enjoying life. You should be going on a cruise, or learning to play the piano, or lying on the beach reading a good book. Not spending your precious time learning about Medicare on a confusing government Website.

Serious Questions

So... Let's say you spend four hours on the Medicare.gov website and you now have a basic understanding of Medicare, let me ask you this:

- Do you know what Medicare plan you are going to enroll in?
- Did you sift through the 50 to 100 Medicare Plans available in your area?
- Do you know the difference between a *Medicare Supplement plan* and an *HMO Medicare Advantage Plan?*

If you answered yes, you are definitely in the minority. Most people who are eligible for Medicare are totally confused and don't know how to go about choosing the correct Medicare plan for themselves.

Let's take a look at three of the *biggest mistakes* eligible Medicare beneficiaries make prior to enrolling in a Medicare plan.

Diane Daniels

1. Wait Till It's Too Late

You may think that having several months to enroll in Medicare is a piece of cake. Not so. Applications can get lost and humans can make mistakes.

You may have up to six months prior to your 65th birthday to enroll in Medicare. My advice is to take your time to make one very important decision. This will be your health insurance for the rest of your life.

Medicare establishes an *initial enrollment period* for people turning 65 for a reason. If you don't enroll in Medicare during your initial enrollment period, you may be assessed a penalty. Take advantage of that three- to seven-month window and get *educated* about Medicare. How do you get a good education regarding Medicare?

- Go to the Medicare.gov website and learn as much as you can
- Order Pamphlets from the site
- Read about Medicare and the different types of Medicare plans
- Go to seminars hosted by Medicare Advisers with a large portfolio of private insurance carriers (the more Medicare plans offered, the more likely you'll enroll in a plan that fits you)

But best of all (in my humble opinion) you can read this book! If you have questions, please email me at diane@callsamm.com or visit my website at www.callsamm.com

I'm here to *educate* you about Medicare. I *educate* and assist you in finding a Medicare plan that suits your lifestyle best.

2. Take Advice from Family or Friends.

Family members and friends mean well, but let's face it – they're not experts in Medicare. Let's look at what could happen.

Your neighbor Phil tells you he's on XYZ Medicare Advantage plan. Phil says he gets $15 worth of Band-Aids a month for free! Phil believes XYZ Medicare Advantage plan is the best thing since sliced bread and so he thinks you should be on the plan as well. So good old Phil gives you his agent's phone number.

You call Phil's agent who then comes over to tell you all about XYZ Medicare plan. The problem is, Phil's agent is authorized to offer *only* the XYZ Medicare plan. This means you will hear about this one plan, and one plan only. Sounds good enough, and hey, you've always liked Phil, right? So you enroll.

Two years later, you need hip replacement surgery. You want the surgeon from New York City who performed your wife's surgery to do the operation. You call XYZ Medicare plan to make the arrangements. The answer comes back: *Denied*. Sorry, they say, but you'll have to have the operation by an orthopedic doctor in your area.

Didn't see that coming, did you?

If I needed to install a ceiling fan, I would never attempt to run wires through the ceiling on my own. I'd call an electrician, because he's the expert – and I know nothing about electricity and wiring.

The same principle applies when you're enrolling in Medicare or you need to change your Medicare plan. Call a *Medicare Adviser*. A Medicare Adviser with a portfolio of many different insurance carriers will be able to offer you a Medicare plan that will individually suit your needs.

3. Enrolling in a Medicare Advantage Plan with Little or No Out-of-pocket Expenses

Let's say that you read an advertisement in the Sunday paper announcing a Medicare Seminar coming up at a local restaurant. It's the annual enrollment period, and you remember that's the time you can change Medicare plans. The seminar is hosted by the *ABC Medicare Company* and they're offering every attendee *free pie and coffee.* You call the number and make your reservation. You want to learn more about Medicare and the changes coming up for the new year.

At the seminar the agent discusses Medicare and the ABC Medicare plan. The agent tells you that their ABC Medicare plan has little or no co-pays for your medical care. You had co-pays for almost all your treatment on your current Medicare plan. You look up your doctor's in the ABC Medicare plan directory. All three doctors are on the plan! You'll be saving so much money. You're sold. You enroll in the ABC Medicare plan right after the seminar.

The next July, you and your wife travel on a cruise to the Mediterranean. You've been waiting for this trip for a lifetime! During the cruise, your wife has chest pain and has to be airlifted to a hospital in Greece. She is admitted for a heart attack and is released four days later.

Back home, you call the ABC Medicare plan to discuss reimbursement. The customer representative looks up your benefits and advises you that you don't have coverage outside of the United States for emergency treatment. You're staring at your Visa statement. The total bill for the hospital stay in Greece is over $45,000.00. *Yikes!*

Didn't see that coming, did you?

It's imperative that you understand *all* the benefits of your Medicare plan. There are many Medicare plans that

The Medicare Survival Guide

would have provided emergency treatment coverage outside the United States. Because you were *captivated* with this plan's *little or no* out-of-pocket expenses, you didn't realize your benefits were *limited* to the United States *only*!

Find a Plan that Fits

It's important to find the Medicare plan that fits your lifestyle and needs. Medicare coverage can be compared to buying fruit. Let's say you buy a bag of McIntosh apples. When you purchase them in a bag you'll pay a cheaper price, but, you can't see *all* the apples. You assume that all the apples in the bag look like the ones you *can* see.

If you buy an *individual* McIntosh Apple, you see the size of the apple, the color and you can feel how firm it is. You'll pay more in price, because you know it's better than the bag of apples. However, you still don't know how much pesticide was used on the apple or if it was waxed from last season.

Now, you see the *organic* McIntosh Apples. The sign tells you the apples were picked at *Joe's* local orchard where no pesticides are used. Only natural organic materials were used to grow the apples. It took just 48 hours from the tree to the market. Your mouth is watering. Those are awesome apples. You'll pay a higher price for the *organic* apples, but to you, it's worth it. You know *exactly* what you're buying. You bite into an *organic* apple and it's delicious!

Medicare plans are similar. You can enroll in a Medicare Advantage HMO plan that has *little or no* co-pays. The network will be *limited*. You will not be able to receive medical treatment anywhere you'd like. This experience is like buying the bag of McIntosh apples.

You may enroll in a Medicare Advantage PPO plan that has higher out-of-pocket expenses, but it gives you a larger network of providers. This experience is like buying the single McIntosh apple.

You may enroll in a Medicare Supplement plan where you will pay a monthly premium, but you'll be able to be treated *anywhere* in the United States that accepts Medicare. Any doctor – any hospital, which accepts Medicare. You won't be asked to pay *any* additional co-pays or co-insurance. This is like buying the organic McIntosh apple. *Simply scrumptious!*

Making a mistake in regards to the Medicare plan you enroll in can be detrimental. Seek the advice of a Medicare Adviser with a large portfolio to assist in educating you about Medicare before you enroll!

I wrote this book because the demand for Medicare education is tremendous. I speak daily to Medicare beneficiaries who didn't even realize they had *choices* in Medicare plans. This book will give you an overview of Medicare and an understanding of the different types of Medicare plans. I'll share stories about clients (the names are changed to protect the innocent) and their Medicare experiences – both good and bad. I'll provide some tips to help you save out-of-pocket expenses. I'll arm you with my contact information if you need to ask further questions or make a comment.

My goal is to *educate* you about Medicare. You need a basic foundation to build upon. This book will do just that. If you need more specific information about Medicare, visit my website – www.callsamm.com or call a SAMM Advisor at 855-855-7266.

Now, sit back and dig into your Medicare Survival Guide and arm yourself with knowledge.

CHAPTER 1

The History of Medicare

Today, nearly 50 million Americans depend on Medicare for their health insurance coverage. That amounts to about 15 percent of the nation's population.

Medicare is the Federal Health Insurance Program for people age sixty-five and older, as well as people with certain disabilities, and people with end stage renal disease (a.k.a. kidney failure). The program is administered by the Federal government and financed through payroll taxes and fees paid by the beneficiaries themselves.

In 2015, Medicare will be celebrating its 50th Birthday. It's hard to imagine that 50 short years ago, Americans over the age of 65 were on their own to pay for healthcare. I can't fathom the fact my grandparents paid for their own healthcare, during a time they needed help the most. These were the same men who fought in a massive war while the nation slept at night, and the women on the home front ran the home and raised the children. I'm glad my grandparents lived to receive benefits from Medicare. My parents are receiving Medicare benefits, and I'm looking forward to the benefits of Medicare when I turn 65.

In my Brooklyn memories, I can remember my great-grandmother, Nanny, at the first of every month watching out the front windows, eagerly awaiting the mailman.

"Check should be coming today," she'd say.

Pretty soon I would hear, "Hear he comes!" Hurrying to the front door, she went out on the stoop to wait. I could hear her trading cordial words with the mailman. Shen then closed the door, walked to her favorite green chair, sat down and riffled through the mail until she found what she was looking for.

"Here it is," she shouted. I knew what was coming next; this was a ritual I'd seen many times before. Pulling the check from the envelope, Nanny stood up to dance a little jig. "I love you my baby boy," she sang.

Nanny kissed the check and then held it close to her cheek and fondled it like it was a newborn. "Thank you for everything, my boy."

Nanny was talking about her youngest son Tommy. I never met my great-uncle Tommy, but I knew much about him. At the young age of 19, he enlisted into WWII where he served as a bombardier in the Air Force. He flew 19 missions after which he'd written to Nanny telling her he was on his way home. He had one more mission – one he volunteered for. That was his last mission; Tommy never made it home. His plane was shot down over Germany.

Nanny had no pension; she had no money in annuities or investments, so quite literally that monthly check helped Nanny survive.

Today, in a similar fashion, Medicare has become a life-saving factor for many of our senior citizens. In this chapter, we'll take a look at how all of this came about.

(**NOTE:** From an early age, my Nanny taught me to respect veterans. She impressed upon me the high price they paid for our basic freedoms in this country. Stories about Uncle Tommy helped me appreciate what freedom truly means. Nanny helped me to become aware that I was free to play outside, or I could watch TV, I could attend the church of my choice, and I could be whatever I chose to be when I grew up – all because of those who were brave enough to defend that freedom. That honor and respect remains with me to this day. Thank you, veterans.)

Signed into Law

On July 30, 1965, President Lyndon Baines Johnson signed Medicare into law under Title XVIII of the Social Security Act. The signing ceremony took place in Independence, Missouri at the Truman Library.

Former President Harry S. Truman sat at the table while the law was signed.

President Johnson held the ceremony there to honor Truman's leadership on health insurance, which he first proposed in 1945. President Truman had attempted to bring Medicare to fruition during his presidency, but there wasn't enough support. President Kennedy picked up the ball and ran with it. President Johnson signed Medicare into law. President Truman was also the first beneficiary to enroll in Medicare; however, he wouldn't start receiving his benefits until July of 1966.

Two Parts to Original Medicare

The original Medicare had two main components – Part A and Part B. Part A included *inpatient* hospital services and Part B included *outpatient* services.

Medicare services didn't actually begin until July 1, 1966. More than 19 million American citizens were eligible to enroll. 93% of those Americans enrolled in the Medicare program that took a little over a year to begin services. It wasn't easy to persuade the first qualified beneficiaries of the Medicare program to enroll. According to an article written by Washington Post journalist, William Raspberry, the government hired over two thousand workers to go door-to-door in an attempt to enroll Americans aged sixty-five and older.

The earliest Medicare beneficiaries paid a $40 deductible for Part A.

After a beneficiary paid their Part A deductible, Medicare would pick up the remaining bill for medically needed services. After a beneficiary's annual Part B deductible was paid, the beneficiary would pay 20% of the Medicare allowable services and Original Medicare would pay the remaining 80%.

Moving forward to present day, beneficiaries pay a $1,216.00 deductible for Part A.

Part A, the *inpatient insurance,* is provided at no charge to most eligible beneficiaries. Part A is funded by revenue from a 2.9% payroll tax levied on employers, employees, and the self-employed. Part A of Original Medicare is also funded when Original Medicare beneficiaries pay their deductibles and co-insurances for treatment.

Beneficiaries who voluntarily enrolled in Part B paid a monthly premium of $3.00, which President Truman paid with his enrollment. This was estimated to be enough to fund 50 percent of Part B costs, and federal general revenues covered the remainder.

Part B is for *outpatient services*. Part B covers services such as - doctor visits, x-rays, blood draws and outpatient surgery. I will talk more about Part B services in Chapter 2. Currently, beneficiaries whose income is less than eighty-five thousand dollars a year, pay a monthly premium of $104.90.

In 2006 a surtax was added to the Part B premium for higher-income seniors (annual incomes over $85,000.00). Below lists the 2015 Part B monthly premiums for an individual.

If your annual income is:

a. Over $85,000 dollars up to $107,000 dollars - Your Part B Premium is $146.90
b. Over $107,000 dollars up to $160,000 dollars - Your Part B Premium is $209.80
c. Over $160,000 dollars up to $214,000 dollars - Your Part B Premium is $272.70
d. Over $214,000 dollars -Your Part B Premium is $335.70

You can contact Social Security to determine your Part B Premium.

Notable Amendments

The Social Security Amendments of 1972 authorized an expansion of Medicare. The act granted benefits to those people under 65 who receive Social Security disability cash payments for at least 24 months. The act also added people with end-stage renal disease who require maintenance dialysis or a kidney transplant.

The Balanced Budget Act of 1997 was signed into law by President Clinton on August 5, 1997. Beneficiaries could remain in the Original Medicare program or enroll in the newly formed Medicare *Part C,* "Medicare + Choice" privatized by health insurance management. Medicare + Choice began to offer expanded private plan options to Medicare beneficiaries.

The Medicare Modernization Act of 2003 was signed by President George W. Bush. Medicare Part D, also called the Medicare Prescription drug benefit, began in January 2006. Medicare Part D helped subsidize the costs of prescription drugs and prescription drug insurance premiums for Medicare Beneficiaries.

Another Interesting Fact About Part A

Medicare funds the vast majority of medical school residency training in the US. This tax-based financing covers resident salaries and benefits through payments called *Direct Medical Education* or DME payments. Medicare supports teaching hospitals with over $8 billion per year for their Graduate Medical Education, while Medicaid funds over $2 billion. The Department of Defense, the Veterans Administration, and private payers also pay for portions of resident physician education.[*]

Medicare also uses funds for *Indirect Medical Education* or IME payments, a subsidy paid to teaching hospitals that is tied to admissions of Medicare patients in exchange for training resident physicians in certain selected specialties.

Next time you visit your primary physician, ask them where they did their residency. If the hospital is a *teaching* hospital it's more than likely Medicare helped pay for your doctor's residency program.

Now that we've covered a brief history of Medicare, let's take a more in-depth look at the different Parts of Medicare.

*COGME Fifteenth Report. Financing Graduate Medical Education in a Changing Health Care Environment. Rockville, Md: U.S. Department of Health and Human Services; December 2000

CHAPTER 2

Do You Know Your A, B, C and Ds?

PART A

The Hospital Insurance

Sarah Kellogg Contacts Me

A lady named Sarah Kellogg contacted me asking for assistance concerning her 70-year-old husband, Jack. Sarah is 62 and still works full-time as a medical receptionist at a private practice, but she's getting ready to retire in six months. Sarah's current private health insurance includes Jack on the policy. Her dilemma is that she doesn't know what to do for Jack when her private insurance policy ends at retirement.

"Has Jack enrolled in Medicare?" I asked.

"He's enrolled in Part A, but not Part B," Sarah told me.

"How long has Jack been on your employer's health insurance plan?"

"For the past twelve years."

"That's great!" I said.

Since Jack has already turned 65, he's entitled to enroll in the Medicare program. I learned Jack had worked for ten consecutive years and paid FICA taxes. That entitles him to enroll in Medicare Part A with *no* premiums attached. He can enroll in Medicare Part A, but Part B is *optional*. If Jack wishes to enroll in Part B, he'll be required to pay a monthly premium (currently at $104.90 a month). Jack will also be required to pay the annual deductible of $147.00 *before* Part B benefits kick in. Jack will be responsible for 20% of the Medicare allowable bill. Medicare will pay the remaining 80%.

Deferring Part B

Jack is on credible health care coverage by being on Sarah's policy. That allows him to *defer* enrolling in Part B until he comes off of Sarah's policy – with no penalties.

Jack will have no outpatient health insurance when he comes off of Sarah's policy. This means his best decision is to enroll in Part B. I advise Jack to contact his local Social Security office and make an appointment to enroll in Medicare Part B.

Once Jack receives his new Medicare ID card, which identifies he's enrolled in Medicare Part A and Part B, I'll then be able to sit with Jack and go over his options. I'll assist him in choosing a Medicare Plan that will suit his needs.

The Importance of Timeliness

Timeliness is of the utmost importance when applying for Medicare. Since Sarah Kellogg contacted me six months prior to her retirement, I was able to help Jack enroll in Medicare Part B with no penalties. I can now help him review his other Medicare options in order to find the one Medicare Plan that will fit him best.

The Kelloggs avoided a disastrous mistake that people often make when it comes to Medicare – that is the mistake of not contacting a Medicare Adviser early enough! If they had waited to contact me after Sarah came off her employer's health insurance policy, Jack would have had only eight months to complete his enrollment in Part B. In that amount of time you run into the risk of having paperwork lost, or dealing with delays in the Medicare system. Penalties would have been looming.

Sarah was concerned about Jack and took action by making preparations prior to her retirement. Sarah will purchase an individual short-term plan for herself until she reaches her eligibility for Medicare.

This was a good ending for the Kelloggs.

You're on Original Medicare! Congratulations! You're 65 years old and you have health insurance. But do you really understand what that means for you?

The simple explanation is that Medicare will pay the majority of your Medicare allowable bill. You'll pay the remainder of the bill. Medical care is not totally free of charge. It never was and it never will be.

Part A

Part A is the *inpatient insurance* of Medicare. This means when you're admitted to a hospital for medically necessary treatment, or you're admitted to a skilled nursing facility, or a Medicare-approved hospice facility, Part A of Medicare pays your medically necessary bill – after you've paid your deductible.

You don't have to pay a monthly or annual premium for Part A of Medicare as long as you contributed to payroll taxes for ten consecutive years, or paid into payroll taxes for forty quarters during your lifetime. Anyone whose spouse earned work credits will qualify for Medicare Part A also. Working all those years and paying into the separate hospital insurance fund, entitles you to Part A of Medicare at no additional premium.

Individuals who are ineligible for premium-free Part A coverage can enroll voluntarily by paying a monthly premium, if they also enroll in Part B. This is called *Medicare Buy-In*. You'll pay up to $407.00 per month. Penalties for late enrollment may apply.

Deductibles

Part A has deductibles. Each time you're admitted into the hospital for a medically necessary reason, and the number of admitted days is less than sixty consecutive days, you will pay a Part A deductible of over $1,000.00.

If you're admitted into the hospital, then released and you remain out of the hospital for at least sixty consecutive days, and then need to be admitted for a previous or new condition, you'll be billed a new deductible Part A charge.

First Things First

But let's take first things first. In 2015, you have a deductible over $1,000.00 if you are admitted to the hospital. You will pay the deductible for being admitted to the hospital as an *inpatient* <u>every single time</u> if each admission is sixty days apart. If you are admitted to the hospital *less* than sixty days apart, with the same diagnosis, you will *not* have to pay the deductible again. Medicare will pay the majority of your medically needed bill after you pay your deductible. You will *not* owe the remaining cost of the bill. Let's look at an example:

John is admitted into the hospital for chest pain. John spends three days in the hospital and has several tests. John has an echocardiogram, a catheterization test and an ultrasound of his heart. John is released from the hospital. Three weeks later, John receives a bill from the hospital for $33,000.00. John pays his current deductible of $1,216.00. Medicare will pay the pre-determined part of the bill. John will not receive an outstanding bill for any other medically necessary charges. If John is re-admitted to the hospital for the same condition in less than sixty days, he will not be charged another bill for medically necessary treatment as long as his hospital stay does not go over sixty days.

If John is admitted to the hospital for a new illness or injury within sixty days of his release from the hospital, he *will* pay his deductible all over again.

Confused yet? Let's try another example:

Poor John! Just three months later, he has a severe stroke and is admitted to the hospital again. This time, John has serious consequences due to the stroke and is admitted to the hospital for 63 days.

John will owe his Part A hospital deductible of $1,216.00. This is a new illness. The hospital bill is $150,000. Medicare will pay for the pre-determined part of the bill. John was admitted to the hospital for over 60 days. John will have to pay **$315.00** a day for each day that he is admitted to the hospital over sixty days. John stayed 63 days. John will owe the hospital $945.00 for being an inpatient for days 61 through 63.

Original Medicare can get quite expensive. There is no cap on the out-of-pocket expenses you will pay during the year. You will pay a Part A hospital deductible each time you are admitted into the hospital up to sixty consecutive days. When you're released, if you stay out of the hospital as an inpatient for less than sixty consecutive days, you will not have to pay the hospital deductible again. You will continue counting your inpatient days in the hospital from where you left off.

John spent sixty-three days as a hospital inpatient for a stroke. If he is admitted into the hospital 44 days later with another stroke, he will continue his hospital days from where he left off. He will not pay an additional deductible. John will pay $315.00 for each day he is admitted between days 60-90.

What Services Does Part A Cover?

When you're admitted to a hospital, Medicare Part A hospital insurance will cover the following for a limited time:
- A semiprivate room; or a private room if medically necessary
- All meals, including special, medically required diets
- Regular nursing services
- Special care units, such as intensive care and coronary care
- Drugs, medical supplies, and appliances furnished by the facility, such as casts, splints, wheelchair
- Hospital lab tests, x-rays, and radiation treatment billed by the hospital
- Operating and recovery room costs
- Blood transfusions (you pay for the first three pints of blood, unless you arrange to have them replaced by an outside donation of your blood to the hospital)
- Rehabilitation services, such as physical therapy, occupational therapy, and speech pathology, provided while you are in the hospital

Medicare Part A hospital insurance *does not cover*:
- Personal convenience items such as television, radio, or telephone
- Private duty nurses
- A private room when not medically necessary

Will the Part A hospital deductible be raised in the coming years? Historically, yes. The final decision will be determined by the Center for Medicare and Medicaid Services (a.k.a. CMS) later in 2015.

Skilled Nursing Facility (SNF)

What happens if you have to be admitted into a skilled nursing facility? What is a skilled nursing facility you may ask? A skilled nursing facility is defined by CMS as:

A nursing facility with the staff and equipment to give skilled nursing care and, in most cases, skilled rehabilitative services and other related health services.

Eligibility for Skilled Nursing Facility (SNF)

You're eligible for a SNF if you meet all of these conditions:
- You have Part A and have days left in your benefit period (up to 90 consecutive days per benefit period or using Lifetime Days (maximum of 60 days lifetime).
- You have a *qualifying hospital stay* (admitted for three days). The day you are dismissed is not counted.
- Your doctor has decided that you need daily skilled care given by, or under the direct supervision of, skilled nursing or rehabilitation staff. If you're in the SNF for skilled rehabilitation services only, your care is considered daily care even if these therapy services are offered just 5 or 6 days a week, as long as you need and get the therapy services each day they're offered.
- The services you receive are in a SNF that's certified by Medicare.

- You need these skilled services for a medical condition that was either:
  1. A hospital-related medical condition.
  2. A condition that started while you were getting care in the skilled nursing facility for a hospital-related medical condition.

What Services Are Covered In a Skilled Nursing Facility?

Medicare-covered services include, but aren't limited to:
- Semi-private room (a room you share with other patients)
- Meals
- Skilled nursing care
- Physical and occupational therapy
- Speech language services
- Medical social services
- Medications
- Medical supplies and equipment used in the facility
- Ambulance Transportation (when other transportation endangers health) to the nearest supplier of needed services that aren't available at the SNF.
- Dietary Counseling

Another *inpatient facility* covered by Part A of Medicare is Hospice.

Hospice

Hospice is defined by CMS as a special way of caring for people who are terminally ill. Hospice care involves a team-oriented approach that addresses the medical, physical, social, emotional, and spiritual needs of the patient. Hospice also provides support to the patient's family or caregiver.

Part A will cover the majority of cost related to a Medicare-certified hospice care program. Patients may only receive care from one hospice program at a time.

In addition, a physician and the hospice medical director must verify that you have a terminal illness, meaning you are documented as having less than six months to live.

You must also sign a statement which states you choose hospice care instead of standard Medicare covered benefits. Medicare will continue to cover health issues that are not related to the terminal illness as outlined in your benefit manual.

Be sure to research the amount of services that will be provided if you decide to have hospice care at home, before you agree to give up standard Medicare benefits. Some services are limited. Nursing visits could be as little as one hour every other day. Do your due diligence!

Duration of Hospice

Medicare generally covers a total of 210 days of hospice care. This is broken into two 90-day periods of benefits which is followed by a 30-day period. Each of the periods may be extended, but only when a doctor recertifies that your condition remains terminal. In some rare and extenuating circumstances, coverage may be extended indefinitely with the proper support and documentation from your physician(s).

Hospice Care is usually given in your home. The focus on hospice is on *comfort* and not on curing an illness. These services are included under Medicare Part A when your

doctor includes them in the palliative care (for comfort) plan, for your terminal illness and related condition(s):
- Doctor services
- Nursing care
- Medical equipment (like wheelchairs or walkers)
- Medical supplies (like bandages and catheters)
- Drugs for symptom control or pain relief (may need to pay a small copayment)
- Hospice aide and homemaker services
- Physical and occupational therapy
- Speech-language pathology services
- Social work services
- Dietary counseling
- Grief and loss counseling for you and your family
- Short-term inpatient care (for pain and symptom management)
- Short term respite care (may need to pay a small copayment)
- Any other Medicare-covered services needed to manage your pain and other symptoms related to your terminal illness, as recommended by your hospice team.

What You Pay For Hospice Care

Medicare pays the hospice provider for your hospice care. There is no deductible. You will have to pay the following:

No more than $5 for each prescription drug and other similar products for pain relief and symptom control.

Five percent of the Medicare-approved amount for inpatient respite care at a Medicare approved hospice facility.

What is Respite Care?

Respite care is defined by Medicare as temporary care provided in a nursing home, hospice inpatient facility, or hospital so that a family member or friend who is the patient's caregiver can rest or take some time off. Respite care can be an important part of the hospice plan.

How to Learn More about Hospice

Go to the Medicare website: www.medicare.gov and put *hospice* in the search bar.

You can call the *National Hospice Association* at (703) 837-1500, or go to their website: www.nhpco.org

Not it's time to move on and take a look at Part B of Medicare.

Part B

The Outpatient Services

As I have pointed out previously, you can think of Part A as being the part of your policy that covers inpatient needs, whether in a hospital, skilled nursing facility, (SNF) or a hospice facility. Part B, then, covers just about everything else.
- Doctor visits come under Part B
- Having blood drawn is under Part B
- Going to physical therapy is under Part B
- Having same day surgery at an outpatient facility is covered under Part B
- The majority of your medical care will fall under Part B of Medicare

Part B covers two types of services – Medically necessary services and preventive services.

Medically necessary services are services or supplies needed to diagnose or treat your medical condition. The services must also be accepted standards of medical practice.

Preventative services refer to health care to prevent illness (pneumonia for example),or to detect it at an early stage (cancer for example). Early prevention is when treatment is most likely to work best.

Some of the more common Preventative services under Medicare are:
  a. Having a blood test to check cholesterol and triglyceride levels is free of charge if done every five years.
  b. Having a bone density test –
     1. If prescribed by a physician and a person's x-ray shows *possible* osteoporosis or a vertebral fracture.

2. A person is diagnosed with *hyperthyroidism.*
   3. A person taking *prednisone* as a steroid treatment plan.
   4. A woman who is *estrogen* deficient or at risk for osteoporosis.
 c. A colonoscopy
   1. Covered every 2 yrs. If the individual is at high risk for colorectal cancer.
   2. Covered every 10 yrs. If the individual is at average risk for colorectal cancer.
 d. A Mammogram
 e. Prostate Cancer Screening
 f. Preventative Shots
   1. Flu
   2. Hepatitis B
   3. Pneumonia

Other preventative services can be found on my website, www.callsamm.com

Durable Medical Equipment (DME) is covered under Part B. Some examples of supplies (but not limited to) needed to diagnose or treat your medical conditions are:
- Wheelchair
- Walkers
- Oxygen
- Diabetic monitors

You can determine if your item, service, or supply is covered by Medicare by going to the Medicare.gov website:
   http://www.medicare.gov/coverage/your-medicare-coverage.html

Contact your Medicare health plan and speak to someone who can verify if an item is covered. You can also call Medicare at 800-633-4227.

You can see the tremendous amount of coverage under Part B of Medicare. That's why enrolling in Part B of Medicare is optional. Paying a monthly premium will cover you to pay 20% of the Medicare approved bill. Medicare will pay the other 80%. Let's look at an example.

John is referred to a cardiologist for follow-up treatment. The cardiologist visit will cost a total of $350.00. John has an annual deductible for Part B, currently at $147.00. John pays his deductible of $147.00. Now John is able to utilize his Part B benefits.

Medicare will pay 80% of the pre-determined part of the bill. For the example, let's say Medicare will pay on $300.00. Medicare will pay 80%, which is $240.00. John is responsible for the remaining 20% of the $300.00, which is $60.00. The physician's office is *not* allowed under law to bill you the remaining $50.00 for his services (a.k.a. *excessive charges*). The doctor has agreed to a contract with Medicare to accept the amount for his services.

Original Medicare has no cap on out-of-pocket expenses. Every time you need medical treatment whether at a doctor's office, having blood drawn, or having an x-ray at a free-standing facility, you will pay 20% of the Medicare approved cost. You will keep paying annual deductibles, and 20% of the Medicare approved bills – always.

Talking about Medicare Part B reminds me of one of my clients who didn't understand Medicare Part A or Part B.

I received a phone call from a woman named Janet who started by telling me she was turning 65 in two months and she wasn't sure what she needed to do to enroll in Medicare.

Janet told me she was referred to me by her church friend, Bea, who happens to be one of my clients. Bea told Janet to call me and tell me her concerns about Medicare and that I would help her with any problems.

I asked Janet if we could meet in person. Because Janet didn't know me I wanted her to feel comfortable discussing her concerns in a comfortable, private environment. Janet was delighted to meet with me so we scheduled an appointment. Janet was interested in discussing Medicare Advantage Plans. It is a Medicare regulation that an individual *shall* sign a *scope of appointment* form prior to when a licensed insurance Agent will discuss Medicare Advantage Plans with an individual. I met with Janet prior to our scheduled appointment, explained the form to Janet and had her sign the scope of appointment form. It is a requirement for each licensed insurance agent to hold on to the signed scope of appointment for a period of *ten years.* I'm serious!

It was a blistering hot August day in Florida. (Then again, how else would it be? August in Florida is one word – miserable! When I'm feeling miserable because of the heat and humidity in Florida, I miss Brooklyn.)

When I met with Janet I learned that she lived in a duplex within a fifty-five plus community. All the houses look the same. Nothing extravagant, but very cute. There was a small front patch of grass with a sidewalk leading to the front door. A parking spot was neatly laid out next to the patch of grass. One car per unit, Janet had informed me. Since she didn't own a car she told me to park in that spot.

As I got out of my car, she opened her front door. "Hi there," she called out. "How are you Diane."

I smiled and answered, "Hi Janet. Good to see you."

Janet doesn't look a day over fifty. She was dressed in a light-colored blouse and slacks with her hair tied up in a kerchief. She ushered me inside. "Sit down and take a load off your feet."

I looked for the kitchen or dining room table with chairs. I always try to sit in an individual chair at a table. (I've had some really bad experiences with bed bugs and fleas in the past.) No table and chairs to be found so.... reluctantly I sat on the sectional sofa in the living room. Janet sat a cushion's-width away from me.

"I want to thank you for reaching out to me for assistance, Janet," I told her.

"Bea says you're her Earth angel," Janet said. "That means since I trust Bea I can trust you!"

"Bea's a special lady," I said, thankful that we were already at this trust level. "Tell me how I can help you."

"Bea said you helped her find a Medicare plan that really fit her lifestyle. I'd like for you to do the same for me. I don't understand Medicare at all."

(This certainly wasn't the first time I'd ever heard that statement.)

"I want to help you have a better understanding of Medicare, Janet, and I also want to assist you in finding the Medicare plan that fits you best. So let's get started."

I began by asking Janet a few general questions about her income, her overall health, and if she had received her Medicare red, white and blue card.

The Medicare Survival Guide

"Yes. I did," she said. "Let me get it for you." Janet dug in her purse to get her Medicare identification card and handed it to me.

I looked at the card and took note of her name, social security number, and Medicare effective dates. Her Medicare Part A effective date was October 1. Janet's effective date for Medicare Part B was listed as *not applicable.* I asked Janet if she had enrolled in Medicare Part B.

"No," she replied. "The man from the insurance company sat right here and told me not to sign up for Part B."

I tried to disguise my surprise. "I don't understand. What man from what insurance company told you not to enroll in Part B?"

"An insurance man from Medicare."

"Medicare would not send anyone to your home," I told her. "Do you have a business card from this insurance man?"

"No. He didn't leave a business card. He told me he'd call me back in October."

I went over a few Medicare regulations regarding soliciting with Janet. "Medicare would not send any employee to knock at your door unannounced. Any insurance agent who wishes to speak to a prospective client about Medicare Advantage plans would have to set up a prior appointment, like we did."

From there, she and I went over a few more Medicare regulations regarding soliciting until Janet had a good understanding.

Through our conversation, I learned Janet didn't have any type of pension or Veteran benefits. She didn't have any other assets and her income was below the poverty level. Fortunately she was very healthy and didn't take any prescribed medications. Even though she was turning 65 in a couple of months, she looked fantastic.

After completing my Medicare assessment, I had good news for Janet. "You may be entitled to participate in the Medicare Savings Program," I explained. "If you qualify, The Medicare Savings Program would pay for your Medicare Part B monthly premium which currently is $104.90. You'd also be entitled to extra help with any prescription drugs you need medically."

"Really?" Janet sounded surprised. "No one ever told me about that program."

(This is why I love what I do. It really irks me that there isn't enough education out there for Medicare beneficiaries.)

"You'll have to enroll in Medicare Part B to fill out an application for the Medicare Savings Program."

"Let's do it," Janet replied.

A month later, Janet was enrolled in Medicare Part B and accepted into the Medicare Savings Program. She would now enjoy the relief of not having to pay her Medicare Part B premium of $104.90. Additionally, she'd be able to save money on any medically needed prescription drugs.

Next, I assisted Janet in enrolling in a Medicare–Medicaid plan. Medicaid would pay all her out-of-pocket medically needed expenses. Making less than one thousand dollars a month, Janet would not have to sacrifice anything else in order to have proper healthcare.

And again I say, this is why I love my job. I enjoy educating people about Medicare. I truly enjoy finding the Medicare Plans that fit individuals best.

PART C

Medicare Advantage
The "Pay As I Go" Medicare Plan

Medicare-Approved Private Insurance Company

Medicare Advantage plans are not part of Original Medicare. They are **Part C** of Original Medicare. The plans are highly regulated by the Department of Health and Human Services. Medicare Advantage plans must include the same benefits and services covered under Part A and Part B of Original Medicare. The management of the plan is transferred to a Medicare-approved private insurance company. Medicare pays the Medicare-approved private insurance company to manage each Medicare beneficiary they have on their plan. The Medicare Advantage plans usually include Medicare prescription drug coverage (known as an MAPD Plan) as part of the plan. The plans usually include extra benefits and services, in some cases for an extra cost.

Some Medicare Advantage plans do not include prescription drug coverage. These plans might be a good choice for veterans - who visit veteran administration facilities for treatment. It might also be a good choice for individuals who have retirement insurance. Always do your due diligence and check with human resources prior to enrolling in additional plans. You could possibly lose your ability to re-join your retirement insurance program.

Each State has a Department of Insurance which assists in regulating Medicare-approved private insurance companies. Each private insurance company may offer CMS approved Medicare Advantage Plans (MA) and Medicare

Advantage Prescription Drug Plans(MAPD). You can go to www.medicare.gov to look up individual state's Medicare-approved private insurance companies.

No Monthly Premiums

The allure of Medicare Advantage plans is the low, or no, monthly premium. About 17% of Medicare Advantage plans do not charge a monthly premium. The remaining 83% of Medicare Advantage plans currently charge a reasonable monthly premium. The beneficiary is responsible for a co-pay each time they seek medical treatment or a medical test. I call it the *"pay as you go"* plan. Each private insurance plan has its own schedule of co-pays.

As an example, one Medicare-approved private insurance plan may charge a $0 co-pay for each visit to a primary care physician. Another Medicare-approved private insurance plan may charge a $10 co-pay for each primary care physician visit. The benefits for each Medicare-approved insurance plan are relatively the same. The co-pay schedules are different. You can look up individual Medicare-approved insurance plans on the www.medicare.gov website to view the different co-pay schedules. You can also go to my website, www.callsamm.com and request such information.

Unlike Original Medicare, Medicare Advantage plans have an annual out-of-pocket maximum expense. Medicare regulates the cap on annual out-of-pocket expenses. Currently, the maximum annual out-of-pocket expense for each individual is $6,700. Many other Medicare Advantage plans have lower annual out-of-pocket expenses. Some as low as $3,000.00.

Co-Pay Instead of Deductible

There is no Part A deductible included in Medicare Advantage plans. Each individual Medicare-approved insurance plan utilizes its co-pay schedule for days admitted to the hospital. For example:
- One Medicare Advantage plan may charge a $400 per day co-pay for the first three days of admittance.
- A second Medicare Advantage plan may charge $150 per day co-pay for the first five days of admittance.

It's important to research each and every plan in your area to determine the individual plan co-pay schedule. There may be an abundant amount of plans in your area, or there could be less than ten Medicare Advantage plans in your area. Review the current Medicare Advantage booklet you received during enrollment, or go online to www.callsamm.com to review your plan's co-pay schedule.

Network Coverage

Each Medicare-approved private insurance company has their own network of physicians and facilities. Most Medicare-approved private insurance companies provide an HMO network. An HMO network – a *Health Maintenance* Organization is a network of contracted physicians and facilities. The HMO network is relatively associated to where you reside. If you are a resident of New York and you are enrolled on a Medicare Advantage Plan which has an HMO network, you will be required to seek physicians and facilities primarily in your county, city or State. A member who resides in Brooklyn, New York will be required to see a physician in the network who practices in Brooklyn. With prior approval, the member may be approved to see a physician in the Bronx or Manhattan. If the member wanted to see a physician in Buffalo, New York, they may be denied. It is very important for you to determine if your physicians and facilities are in the HMO network, prior to enrolling in the plan. Another issue with an HMO network is a physician may terminate his contract with the private insurance company at any time. A physician's contract is not always signed in January and ends in December. Many physicians enter contracts in mid-year. Let's look at an example.

Dr. Jones signed a provider contract with Medicare Advantage Company X in July of 2014. Dr. Jones decides in February of 2015, that Medicare Advantage X takes an excessive amount of time in paying claims. Dr. Jones advises Medicare Advantage X that he is terminating his contract with them and he will no longer be accepting patients on Medicare Advantage X beginning in April of 2015.

Dr. Jones is *allowed* to terminate his contract mid-year per CMS regulations.

Any patient who see Dr. Jones and are members of Medicare Advantage X Plan, will *no longer* be able to see Dr. Jones beginning April 1, 2015.

Those members will need to find a new physician. They are not permitted to change their Medicare Advantage Plan during the locked-in period (December 8th – October 14th). There are no listed *Special Election Periods* available to these members. These members are literally *stuck* and must find a new physician in the HMO network. During the open enrollment period of 2015 – October 15th – December 7th, the member may change their Medicare Advantage Plan to one Dr. Jones is contracted with. The member will become effective with the new Medicare Advantage Plan on January 1st of 2016. How do you know Dr. Jones won't terminate his contract with the Medicare Advantage Plan you just enrolled in? You don't. Dr. Jones won't tell you either.

CMS has made proposed changes for the 2016 calendar year, regarding keeping provider information current. CMS proposes that Medicare contracted insurance companies communicate with providers at a minimum of four times a year to update information for beneficiaries. The information is to be updated in *real time* on websites. CMS is also considering implementing a nationwide database in 2017, to assist beneficiaries in finding accurate information on providers.

Another type of network in a Medicare Advantage Plan is a PPO (Preferred Provider Organization). A PPO allows its members to see physicians or facilities in a larger area. Sometimes - out of State.

Humana is a private insurance company that has a contract with Medicare. Humana provides CMS approved Medicare Advantage Plans in many different States. Humana has Medicare Advantage Plans that offer an HMO network and Medicare Advantage Plans that offer a PPO network. The Medicare Advantage Plans with a PPO network, allow its members to seek physicians and facilities in the PPO network out-of-state. This may be a plan of choice for a person who resides in a northern State and travels to a southern State during the winter months. That person is known as a *"snowbird"* in Florida. A PPO would allow this person to seek treatment with a physician who is contracted with the Humana PPO network. The PPO plan allows more freedom in regards to physician choice. Therefore, they usually charge higher co-pays for benefits. The co-pay for seeing a primary care physician may cost $10 - $60 on a PPO plan. Physicians are *less* likely to terminate their contracts early with a PPO plan. The physician can see a larger number of patients with a PPO plan. More patients equals more money for a physician.

When you enroll in a Medicare Advantage plan, you *must* see a physician in their own network if you want the Medicare-approved private insurance company to pay your medically necessary bill minus the co-pay. If you decide to see a physician who is not part of the network, you'll be responsible for either a higher co-pay to the doctor or facility, or you may be responsible for the entire bill. A medical emergency is an exception.

If a medical emergency occurs, you will not be charged any additional bill for services covered outside the network, if you were unable to visit an *in-network* facility. You'll still pay your plan's co-pay schedule for each out of network visit. If you see a physician or have procedures done at a facility that's not in the covered network, you'll be responsible for a major portion of the bill. See your Medicare Advantage Plan's detail of benefits to review your responsibility for out of network charges.

Medicare Advantage Prescription Drug Plan

Most Medicare Advantage plans include Prescription Drugs in their plan. They are called Medicare Advantage Prescription Drug plans (MAPD). The majority of Medicare-approved private insurance companies do not charge a premium for the addition of a Prescription Drug plan. Some have a deductible.

Medicare Advantage Prescription Drug Plans have a formulary unique to each plan. The drugs are assigned to a *tier* and each *tier* will determine your co-pay for each drug.

Generic Drugs

Most Medicare Advantage Plans assign Generics to Tier 1 or Tier 2. If you require a prescription for a generic which is assigned to Tier 1, you'll have a co-pay of $0 up to about $15.00, depending upon the Medicare Advantage Plan you're enrolled in. A generic assigned to Tier 2 may have a co-pay of $0 up to about $25.00 depending upon the Medicare Advantage Plan you're enrolled in. Some formularies have added generics through *all* tiers. You must determine what Tier your prescription drugs are on.

An example of a generic drug that is usually assigned to a Tier 1 is *Lisinopril*. *Lisinopril* is a drug used to treat high blood pressure. I have seen *Lisinopril* at a $0 co-pay and at a *$6.00* co-pay. Do your due diligence!

Brand Drugs

Brand drugs are usually assigned to Tier 3 and Tier 4. Brand drugs are name brand drugs, with *no* generics available. An example of a Brand drug is *Tikosyn*. *Tikosyn* is a drug to treat heart arrhythmias. There are currently *no* generic drugs available for *Tikosyn*. That being said, you will pay a higher co-pay for *Tikosyn*. Most formularies will place *Tikosyn* on a Tier 3 or Tier 4.

Formulary Changes

A Medicare Advantage Plan may introduce new drugs into the formulary or remove drugs from the formulary during the plan year. The plan must advise you of the formulary drug change at least 60 days in advance. This gives you ample time to speak with your physician who will assign a different drug for treatment. Your plan may also authorize an additional 31 day refill to assist in the transition. Contact your plan to find out about formulary changes.

Some charge an annual deductible for the addition of a Prescription Drug plan. It's extremely important that you find out if you're paying a monthly premium and or an annual deductible for the addition of a Prescription Drug Plan. Talk to the Medicare agent who enrolled you into the plan or go to my website www.callsamm.com to research plans.

Each Medicare-approved private insurance company has its own schedule of co-pays for each plan. HMO plans have lower co-pays due to the fact that a member is restricted to the number of physicians and facilities in the network. PPO's have larger co-pays due to the fact they have a larger choice of physicians and facilities, some across the entire United States.

It's important to know the co-pay schedule for each Medicare Advantage Plan as well as which physicians and facilities participate in each plan. You may go to www.medicare.gov to research co-pays and physicians in a network, or go to my website at www.callsamm.com

Physicians contracted with Medicare Advantage Plans agree to be paid a certain amount of money per Medicare Advantage patient they see. Physicians must act as the member's health care team captain. The primary care physician completes paperwork, referrals, and preventive exams for each Medicare Advantage patient. When the patient needs to see a specialist, the primary care physician provides the referral and gets it approved from the Medicare Advantage Insurance company.

It's the primary care physician's job to stay in contact with all other health care providers that his patient sees in order to maintain the stream of information from each physician to another. This communication maintains the balance of care for the Medicare Advantage patient and should provide the optimal treatment and services the patient requires. Primary care physicians aren't overly excited that they have so much paperwork to complete and don't get paid for the extra time it takes to complete.

Primary care physicians are leaving many contracts with Medicare Advantage Plans in order to seek better remedies for payment. This sometimes leaves the Medicare Advantage enrollee without the doctor they have been seeing for years. The Medicare Advantage enrollee will have to sign up with a different doctor in the network until they have the opportunity to change Medicare Advantage Plans during the Annual Enrollment Period, which begins on October 15th and ends on December 7th of each year.

Sometimes, the primary care physician doesn't contract with any other Medicare Advantage Plan. This leaves the Medicare Advantage enrollee with the choice of a new doctor or changing to a different type of Medicare plan. This could potentially happen several times annually to a Medicare beneficiary.

This happened to a client who was enrolled in a Medicare Advantage plan – she was losing her primary care physician.

Ellen sent me an email to advise me that her physician, Dr. Gates, was leaving her Medicare Advantage Plan in two months. Ellen liked Dr. Gates and wanted to remain as his patient. Unfortunately for Ellen, it was not during the Annual Enrollment Period for Medicare.

She didn't have any special reason to change her Medicare Advantage plan. Only that her Doctor was not renewing the contract with Ellen's Medicare Advantage Insurance Company. Medicare doesn't consider that reason special. Ellen will have to find a new physician to be her primary care physician for the next nine months. The annual enrollment period will begin in October and Ellen can change to a Medicare Advantage plan that Dr. Gates participates in for January.

Ellen finds a female physician not too far from her residence. Ellen contacts the Customer Service department of her current Medicare Advantage plan and changes primary physicians. I call the new doctor to explain the reason for an appointment. Ellen makes an appointment and sees the new doctor. Ellen is very happy with her.

Two months later, Ellen sends me yet another email. The new female doctor is leaving the Medicare Advantage Plan she's on. Ellen is frustrated and wants to change her Medicare advantage plan. Ellen has no special reason that will allow her to change Medicare Advantage plans at this time. Ellen will have to find a new doctor again. Ellen schedules an appointment with me during October of the next Annual Enrollment Period. Ellen wants to go back to her original physician and wants to change Medicare Advantage Plans.

Ellen and I have worked together for many years. Ellen is frustrated with the system, but understands she is unable to be on a different type of Medicare Plan due to her finances and lifestyle. Ellen knows she can count on me to assist her

The Medicare Survival Guide

in any way I can, when changes to her Medicare Advantage plan affect her.

———

If you decide on a Medicare Advantage plan, you must be prepared for the unexpected. You may lose your physician, your hospital or Medicare may even terminate the plan you're currently on. You must be flexible to be on a Medicare Advantage plan. You must be able to accept the good, the bad and the ugly.

Next we're going to take a look at Part D, Prescription Drugs.

Part D of Medicare

The MMA

Part D of Medicare was added by the Medicare Prescription Drug, Improvement, and Modernization Act (MMA) of 2003. Part D helps pay for prescription drugs not otherwise covered by Part A or Part B.

Beginning in 2006, Part D provided subsidized access to prescription drug insurance coverage on a voluntary basis. Beneficiaries may enroll in either a stand-alone prescription drug plan (PDP), or an integrated Medicare Advantage plan that offers Part D coverage (MAPD).

Enrollment began in late 2005. In 2012, Part D provided protection against the costs of prescription drugs to over 37 million people. Estimated Part D benefits totaled $66.5 billion in 2012.

Part D Fund

The Part D fund is a separate fund to the Part B fund of Medicare. Part D is funded by Medicare.

As a stand-alone prescription drug plan under Part D, there is an initial deductible ($320 in 2015). After meeting the deductible, the beneficiary pays co-pays, up to an initial coverage limit ($2,960 in 2015). A coverage gap starts (commonly known as the *doughnut hole*) after an individual's drug costs reach the initial coverage limit and stops when the beneficiary incurs a certain threshold of out-of-pocket costs ($4,700 in 2015).

A beneficiary entering the coverage gap in 2015 will receive a 55percent manufacturer discount (Brand drugs) from his or her Part D plan for applicable prescription drugs, for a total savings of 55% off the brand drug.

Coumadin

Let's take as an example the brand drug *Coumadin.* There are generic medications available for Coumadin, but many people do best on the brand name drug. Say the total cost for a 30 day supply is $200.00. If you were in the doughnut hole, you would receive a 55% discount off the $200.00 price. Your monthly total for *Coumadin* while in the donut hole would be $90.00. The total cost of a brand drug counts toward your out-of-pocket expenses to reach the next threshold of $4,700. Meaning the entire $200.00 would be applied towards the $4,700.

If you took three other brand drugs, which cost a total of $300.00 a month, plus the $200.00 a month for *Coumadin,* your total out-of-pocket expense for brand drugs would be $500.00. It would take you 9 ½ months at $500 a month to reach the $4,700 level. If you take generic drugs you will receive a 35percent discount from your plan.

Lisinopril

Let's look at an example using the *generic* drug *Lisinopril, and l*et's say *Lisinopril* costs a total of $100 for a 30 day supply. At a 35% discount in the donut hole, you would pay $65.00 for a 30 day supply of *Lisinopril.* The out-of-pocket expense you pay for *Lisinopril* is the amount applied towards the $4,700 plateau. There is no other discount applied. So, $65.00 is counted toward your goal of $4,700 in order to exit the donut hole.

Additional reductions in beneficiary cost sharing in the coverage gap continue in future years so by 2020, the donut hole will be fully phased out. In 2020, the beneficiary will be responsible for 25 percent of prescription drug costs. From our example, the cost of *Lisinopril* was $100.00. Twenty-five percent of $100 is $25.00. In the year 2020, you would pay $25.00 for *Lisinopril*, with no donut hole.

Last Stage

The last stage is called the *Catastrophic Stage*. During this stage, your out-of-pocket expenses for prescription drugs have reached $4,700. For the remainder of the calendar year, you will pay either 5% co-insurance, or a specific co-payment amount ($2.65 in 2015 for generic and $6.60 in 2015 for brand drugs).

For example, the total cost for the generic drug *Furosemide* is $100. A 5% coinsurance would equal $5.00. The copayment amount for generics is $2.65. You would pay the larger amount, which is $5.00 during the catastrophic phase.

A Detailed Look

For a detailed look at the *donut hole*, and catastrophic phases regarding prescription drugs, read your Medicare plan booklet, or go to the SAMM website, www.callsamm.com

Tip for Determining the Donut Hole

You can calculate the yearly cost of your prescriptions to determine if you will enter the donut hole. Call your pharmacy and ask the pharmacist what the Medicare cost of each drug is. For brand drugs, take the total Medicare cost of the drug. (In our brand drug example above, we used *Coumadin*. The total Medicare cost for illustrating our example was $200.00.) Add the monthly total for each prescription brand drug you are taking.

Example:

Brand drug #1 *Coumadin* $200.00
Brand drug #2 $200.00
Brand drug#3 $100.00
Monthly Cost $500.00

Let's say the total Medicare cost for your generic drug is $100.00 (the example we used above was *Lisinopril*). Your out-of-pocket co-pay for a tier 1 generic drug is $3.00 for a thirty day supply.

Under Part D regulations for prescription drugs, your out-of-pocket co-pay and the amount the prescription drug plan pays for your drug may be applied toward the $2,960 threshold.

Example:

Generic drug – *Lisinopril*
Your Monthly Cost $3.00
Plan pays $97.00

Now add the total monthly cost for your brand drugs and your generic drugs:

> Brand Monthly Cost $500.00
> Generic Monthly Cost $100.00
> Total Monthly Cost $600.00

Now add $600.00 x 12 (months) = $7,200.00

With the initial threshold being $2,960, you can calculate when you will reach the initial threshold before twelve months. You'll actually hit the $2,960.00 threshold by May($600.00 x 5 months = $3,000.00) This means you will enter the donut hole, by late May.

Once in the donut hole, you will have a new threshold to reach ($4,700). In the donut hole, you will pay more money out of your pocket for your prescription drugs.

You will receive a 55% discount on the total Medicare cost of brand drugs.

From our example above, you will now pay the following out-of-pocket amount per month while in the donut hole.

Example:

Brand Drug *Coumadin* $90.00 (55% savings of $200.00)
Brand Drug #2 $90.00 (55% savings of $200.00)
Brand Drug#3 $45.00 (55% savings of $100.00)
Total Monthly Amount $225.00

While in the donut hole, you'll pay 65% of the total Medicare cost for generic drugs. In our example above, we used *Lisinopril*. The total Medicare cost for a thirty day supply of *Lisinopril* was $100. You would pay 65% of $100. This would be $65.00.

Now let's add them all together and see what you would pay monthly while in the donut hole.

Brand drugs $225.00
Generic drug $ 65.00
Total $290.00

You would pay $290.00 per month while in the donut hole. That's a lot of money!

The Next Threshold

Your next threshold amount is $4,700.00. What counts towards reaching that threshold?
1. All previous co-pays you've paid for generic and brand drugs, during the initial phase.
2. The 45% co-insurance you pay out-of-pocket and the discount (most of the 55%) amount paid by the plan for brand drugs, while in the donut hole.
3. The 65% you currently pay for each generic drug while in the donut hole.
4. The deductible you have paid towards prescription drugs in the same year.

Where Does That Leave You?

For January, February, March, April, May and half of June, the total paid for Brand drugs was $2,750.

For January, February, March, April, May and half of June, your total out-of-pocket cost for generic drugs was $16.50

This brings the total amount which can be applied toward the $4,700.00 threshold is:

$$\$4,700 - \$2,766.50 = \$1,933.50$$

This means you still need to apply $1,933.50 toward the threshold of $4,700 in order to get out of the donut hole and move into the more affordable catastrophic stage.

If you will be paying $290.00 a month while in the donut hole, you'll reach the $4,700 threshold in late December ($290.00 x 7 = $2,030.00).

You will then reach the next threshold, the catastrophic stage and pay a 5% co-insurance or $6.60 for brand drugs and $2.65 for generic drugs (whichever is more expensive), for the remainder of the calendar year.

In our example, that would look like this:
> Brand drug *Coumadin* - $ 10.00 (5% co-insurance)
> Brand drug #2 - $ 10.00 (5% co-insurance)
> Brand drug #3 - $ 6.60 ($6.60 co-pay for brand drug)
> Generic drug *Lisinopril* - $ 5.00 (5% co-insurance)
> Total Monthly Amount $ 31.60

You will remain in the Catastrophic Stage till the end of December.

January 1st of the new year cleans the slate, and your initial threshold of $2,960.00 will be in place.

There are a few things you can do to prolong reaching the initial $2,960 threshold, which will put you in the donut hole.

1. Ask your physician for samples. Pharmaceutical reps frequently leave samples of medications with physicians to give to their patients. It's a way for patients to try medications first, to see how they react to the medication.
2. Utilize grocery store and pharmacy generic drug savings programs.
   CVS, Safeway, Publix, and Wal-Mart are just a few of the many participating grocery and drug stores utilizing generic drug programs. Go online to your favorite pharmacy or grocery store website to see if they participate in this wonderful program.
   a. Wal-Mart has a $4.00 Generic drug program for a 30 day supply of listed generic drugs. Just tell the pharmacist you'll be using their $4.00

generic drug program and *not* your Medicare insurance card. If your prescription drug is in their formulary, you'll pay just $4.00 for the drug and the cost of the drug won't be added toward the initial threshold of $2,960.

b. Check here to see if your prescription drug is on the Wal-Mart formulary.

http://i.walmartimages.com/i/if/hmp/fusion/customer_list.pdf

3. Contact the pharmaceutical company of your medication.

Many pharmaceutical companies will give you samples or coupons towards purchasing their product.

Many pharmaceutical companies will also offer help in paying for their drugs.

Go to the medicare.gov website to see if your drug company offers help.

http://www.medicare.gov/pharmaceutical-assistance-program/Index.aspx

4. Many States have programs to help pay for drug plan premiums and drug costs. Go to the Medicare.gov website to see if your State participates.

http://www.medicare.gov/pharmaceutical-assistance-program/state-programs.aspx

5. Some local and national charity programs may be able to help with the cost of prescription drugs. Check specific illness charities like the National Organization for Rare Diseases website for information.

http://www.rarediseases.org/

6. If you have a limited income you may receive extra help.

Social Security and Medicare have a program you can apply for if you have limited income and resources.

Check to see if you qualify by going to the social security website.

http://www.ssa.gov/medicare/prescriptionhelp/

For all other assistance with Prescription Drug Plans, go to the Medicare.gov website and research information on under Part D.

http://www.medicare.gov/part-d/index.html

CHAPTER 3

Types of Medicare Plans

Medi-Gap or Supplemental Plan

If you elect to have Original Medicare Part A and Part B, you'll have deductibles and co-insurances as part of the program.

Under Part A as we have previously discussed, you have an inpatient hospital deductible of $1,260.00 for *each* benefit period. Each benefit period lasts sixty days from when you were admitted into the hospital.

If you're released from the hospital and you remain out of the hospital for sixty consecutive days, you have completed one benefit period. If you're admitted into the hospital during the calendar year after the sixty days, you will pay another deductible of $1,260.00.

There is no cap on paying the Part A deductible. January 1st of the new year will wipe the slate clean and your deductible starts all over again.

Under Medicare Part B, you currently have one annual deductible of $147.00. After you have paid your deductible, you will owe 20% of each medically necessary bill for *outpatient* services.

There is no cap on Medicare Part B co-insurance. Each January 1st, the slate is wiped clean and you will owe your Part B deductible all over again.

Each year, CMS determine if your deductibles will be raised. There have been years when the deductible has gone down and there have been years the deductible remained the same. You just don't know.

Medicare Supplement

You have the option to buy a separate policy to provide coverage for the areas Medicare falls short on. This is known as Medicare Supplement or Medicare Supplement Insurance. You buy a Medicare Insurance policy from a private insurance company. When you turn 65 and you enroll in Medicare, you're in your initial enrollment period.

This means you can enroll in Medicare three months prior to your 65th birthday, the month of your 65th birthday, and three months after the month of your 65th birthday. If you decide a Medicare Supplement policy would fit you best, you can enroll up to six months prior to your 65th birthday.

The best part about the initial enrollment period is that you can enroll in a Medicare Supplement Insurance policy *without* any medical underwriting. This means everyone who is turning 65 and in the initial enrollment period is treated the same. There is no discrimination based on prior medical history.

Let's say Mickey, Joe and Roger are all friends. They are all turning 65 in the same year.

Mickey has had two previous heart attacks.

Joe has diabetes and uses insulin

Roger is as healthy as a horse. He runs two marathons a year and plays racquetball every Tuesday and Thursday at the club.

These three men enroll in Medicare Parts A and B during their initial open enrollment. All three men decide they want to purchase a Medicare Supplement policy to provide coverage where Medicare does not. All three men, despite their previous medical histories, will be quoted the same price by Medicare Supplement Company A.

Understanding the Options

This is why it is so important that you understand your options with Medicare. Having no medical underwriting is a huge benefit when deciding on a Medicare Supplement plan. When the initial enrollment period is over – so is the traditional *no-medical-underwriting* benefit. It's a deal that rarely reoccurs.

One exception when no-medical-underwriting would re-appear, is if a Medicare Plan was terminated by Medicare and a beneficiary was forced to look for another plan. That would trigger a Special Election Period, and applying for a Medicare Supplement policy at that time would allow a one-time, no-medical-underwriting benefit due to Medicare terminating the plan, no matter what age you are.

Standardized Benefits

The nice thing about Medicare Supplement policies is that the benefits are standardized. You would be able to purchase a plan in Alaska, Florida or New York and the benefits under the Medicare Supplement policy would be the same. The only states not standardized together are Massachusetts, Minnesota and Wisconsin.

Like Buying a Car

Medicare Supplement plans offer benefits in a similar fashion as buying a car. Let's say you're looking to purchase a 2014 Cadillac ATS. You have three different models to choose from. You can purchase the 2.5 Standard, the 2.0 turbo, or the 3.6 Luxury editions.

If you looked at all three of these cars in the same color side by side, they'd look the same. The difference is in the package. The 2.5 standard has cloth seats and a CD player. The 2.0 turbo gives you faster acceleration and better power steering, in addition to what the 2.5 standard offers. The 3.6 Luxury will give you all leather interior with a Bose stereo touch screen navigation system. The 3.6 Luxury has everything the standard and the Luxury has to offer, plus bells and whistles added on to the same frame that all three models already have.

It's the same idea with Medicare Supplement policies. Each policy starts with the same basic benefits and as you look at each plan, a few features will be added to the policy to build the package.

There are ten model Medicare Supplement plans. Each one is represented by a letter of the alphabet. They start with the letter *A* and end with the letter *N*. (Fancy stuff here.)

Let's take a look at the basic structure of the Medicare Supplement Plan:

Compare Medicare Supplement Plans Side-By-Side

The chart below shows basic information about the different benefits Medicare Supplement policies cover.

Yes = the plan covers 100% of this benefit

No = the policy doesn't cover that benefit

The Medicare Survival Guide

% = the plan covers that percentage of this benefit
N/A = not applicable

Medicare Supplement Benefits	Medicare Supplement Plans									
	A	B	C	D	F*	G	K	L	M	N
Part A coinsurance and hospital costs covered. Plus up to an additional 365 days after Medicare benefits are used	Yes	Yes	Yes	Yes	Yes	Yes	Yes	Yes	Yes	Yes
Part B coinsurance or copayment covered	Yes	Yes	Yes	Yes	Yes	Yes	50%	75%	Yes	Yes***
Blood (The first 3 pints) covered	Yes	Yes	Yes	Yes	Yes	Yes	50%	75%	Yes	Yes
Part A hospice care coinsurance or copayment covered	Yes	Yes	Yes	Yes	Yes	Yes	50%	75%	Yes	Yes
Skilled nursing coinsurance	No	No	Yes	Yes	Yes	Yes	50%	75%	Yes	Yes
Part A Deductible covered	No	Yes	Yes	Yes	Yes	Yes	50%	75%	50%	Yes
Part B deductible covered	No	No	Yes	No	Yes	No	No	No	No	No
Part B excess charges covered	No	No	No	No	Yes	Yes	No	No	No	No
Foreign travel (up to plan limits)	No	No	Yes	Yes	Yes	Yes	No	No	Yes	Yes
Out-of-pocket limit**	N/A	N/A	N/A	N/A	N/A	N/A	$4,940	$2,470	N/A	N/A

* Plan F also offers a high-deductible plan. If you choose this option, you must pay for Medicare-covered costs up to the deductible amount ($2,180 in 2015) before your Medicare Supplement plan pays anything.

** After you meet your out-of-pocket yearly limit **and** your yearly Part B deductible, the Medicare Supplement plan pays 100% of covered services for the rest of the calendar year.

*** Plan N pays 100% of the Part B coinsurance, except for a copayment of up to $20 for some office visits and up to a $50 copayment for emergency room visits that don't result in inpatient admission.

What about the Cost of a Medicare Supplement Plan?

This is where Medicare Supplement plans are very *different*. Each private insurance company has different rates for each Medicare Supplement Policy.

A Medicare Supplement Policy F purchased in Florida with Medicare Supplement ACME Insurance Company, might cost less than the same Medicare Supplement Policy F purchased with the Medicare Supplement ZOO Insurance Company. It is important to purchase a Medicare Supplement Policy with a Medicare Adviser who has a portfolio of different Medicare Supplement carriers to offer you. If you call Medicare Supplement ABC Company, for instance, to get a quote on a Medicare Supplement Policy F, the agent will try to sell you that company Medicare Supplement policy. That's the only insurance company they represent. The agent will make no money if he advised you to contact *Medicare XYZ* company, because the rate might be cheaper at that time. The *ABC* Company Medicare Supplement Policy F has the same benefits as the *XYZ Company* Medicare Supplement Policy F. The *ABC* Medicare Supplement Policy F has a *different* premium than the *XYZ*

Medicare Supplement Policy F. It is imperative for you to check quotes for different Medicare Supplement Policies.

Financial Ratings

Financial ratings are also very important when it comes to Medicare Supplement plans. Standard & Poor (S&P) and Weiss Ratings are companies that uses intelligence to make financial data transparent. S&P and Weiss provides ratings on companies as a tool to evaluate the likelihood that financial obligations by companies will be repaid in full and on time.

An example of an S&P rating for Insurance Financial Strength is AAA. A rating of AAA is the highest rating S&P gives. A company with a AAA rating has an extremely strong capacity to meet its obligations.

On the lower end of the rating scale is D. A company with a financial rating of D has defaulted or will default on its obligations to pay.

In regards to a Medicare Supplement plan, the closer a company is to a AAA rating in Insurance Financial Strength, the higher likelihood the company will pay its claims and on time.

An example of a Weiss Rating for Insurance Financial Strength is A. Rating of A is the highest rating Weiss gives. A company with an A rating from Weiss, offers excellent financial security and has the resources to deal with severe economic conditions.

That's important when you are counting on your Medicare Supplement policy to pay the 20% Medicare allowable cost you owe.

How It Works

As an example, go to the S&P website: http://www.standardandpoors.com/en_US/web/guest/home

In the search box, type the company *United American*. When the company name appears, click on the company name and the site displays a financial strength rating of A+.

According to the S&P definitions, an A+ means United American Insurance Company has a very strong financial strength rating. This is a company I would lean toward doing business with.

Now, go to the Weiss Rating website:
http://www.weisswatchdog.com

Type *United American* in the upper right part of the home page. Check the *insurance companies* bubble, and click on the "search" button.

When the company name appears, click on the company name and the site displays a financial strength rating of B.

According to the Weiss Ratings definitions, a B means United American has good financial security and has the resources to deal with a variety of adverse economic conditions. Again, based on the companies definition of strength ratings, I would lean toward doing business with this company.

Look up your Medicare Supplement company's financial strength rating on the websites to see what their financial strength rating is.

Shopping for Medicare Supplement

I would strongly advise you to do your own due diligence or contact a SAMM Adviser who has a portfolio of Medicare Supplement Insurance plans to offer you. You do not want to call a *specific* Medicare insurance company to speak about their *one* branded Medicare Supplement policies. You will receive quotes for that *one* specific product. Period. If you call Humana and only receive quotes from a Humana representative, you would not know that you could call another company and receive possibly cheaper quotes for the same Medicare Supplement plan.

A Medicare Adviser, who is authorized to offer many Medicare policies from private insurance companies in his portfolio, will be able to offer you the policy that fits you best. Go online and search for a Medicare Adviser in your area. For example, if you live in Pittsburgh, PA, type the words *Medicare Adviser Pittsburgh* in the Google search bar. A number of results will appear with the names of Medicare Advisers in your area who are authorized to offer a portfolio of Medicare policies. If you live in Tampa, FL, type the words *Medicare Adviser Tampa* in the Google search bar. You get the idea. You will also see a list of more common Medicare Insurance Company names.

Watch for Credentials

Start selecting some companies and reviewing the Medicare Adviser's website. The Medicare Adviser should have an area on the website that lists the private Medicare Insurance companies he is authorized to offer. Read that area.

Look for credentials the Medicare Adviser has. Look for national associations like NAMSA (National Association for Medicare Supplement Advisers). A Medicare Adviser who is affiliated with NAMSA had to take a certification exam to be affiliated with NAMSA. They had to take extra training to be a member of NAMSA. NAMSA is a national affiliation. A small percentage of all licensed insurance agents in the United States are members of NAMSA. I am a proud active member of NAMSA. If your Medicare Agent is not affiliated with NAMSA, they should be. NAMSA is an elite association. You should have an elite Medicare Adviser.

Next, go to the area on the website where you can read testimonials. You should be able to read or listen to comments people have made about the Medicare Adviser and company. You may be able to contact some of those people for a reference too. If it's available, contact the person. Tell that person you are looking to enroll in Medicare and you would like to know how the Medicare Adviser from ABC Company helped them. Ask them if they would do business again with that Medicare Adviser. If they say No, thank them and move on to the next listed Medicare Adviser. You want someone who comes with lots of positive testimonials.

Finding the right Medicare Adviser is just as important as finding the Medicare plan that fits you best.

Now we're ready to take a look at the next type of Medicare plan – Medicare Advantage plans.

Medicare Advantage

Another type of private Medicare Insurance plan is the Medicare Advantage Plan. I like to call Medicare Advantage plans the *"pay as you go"* Medicare Plan. Medicare Advantage plans are located under Part C of Medicare. These plans are managed by private insurance companies, contracted with Medicare to manage your Medicare Plan.

At a minimum, they must offer the same benefits as Part A and Part B of Original Medicare. Medicare Advantage plans may add *more* benefits to their plans, but not *less*.

They are regulated under *The Balanced Budget Act of 1997*. Medicare pays a fixed amount to the companies offering Medicare Advantage Plans to manage your health care.

Medicare Advantage plans were introduced to offer beneficiaries more plan options. Most Medicare Advantage plans have little or no monthly premiums. There are usually no deductibles to pay for Part A or Part B benefits. You would pay out-of-pocket co-pays whenever your needed medical services.

Let's create an example. Say you fell down the stairs while carrying the laundry. To break your fall, you put your arms out in front of you as you fell. You hit the bottom landing with your right hand. You hear a snap in your right arm. You immediately feel pain in your arm and can't move it.

You're taken to the nearest emergency room by ambulance. You're given an x-ray of your right arm and diagnosed with a fractured right wrist. A cast is applied to your right wrist and arm. You're given orders to follow up with an orthopedic physician in two weeks. Your son drives you home.

How can you calculate your costs in this situation? Each private insurance company has *different* co-pays for their Medicare Advantage plans.

Let's say you have Medicare Advantage Plan Florida #1. Under this plan, you would look up what your out-of-pocket co-pays are for each benefit you used.

You look up transportation by ambulance and you see your co-pay is $150. You then look up being treated at an emergency room and you find you have a $65 co-pay. Your total *out-of-pocket* cost for today is $215.

When you go see the orthopedic physician in two weeks, you look up specialist visit and see you will pay $45 at that visit.

That's how the Medicare Advantage plan works. Each time you need medical care, you might pay an out-of-pocket co-pay. When you don't need medical care, you don't pay anything. *Pay as you go* health insurance.

Sounds perfect, right?

What are some other criteria for Medicare Advantage plans?

Medicare Advantage plans have networks. A network includes the physicians, hospitals and outpatient facilities you may be treated at. You're not allowed to be treated by just *any* doctor or *any* hospital. You *must* see the physicians, hospitals and outpatient facilities in your insurance plan's network in order for the insurance company to pay your medically necessary bill.

The exception is when you are treated for an emergency. When you are traveling outside your network area and you seek medical treatment for an emergency, you can be treated by an out of network hospital and your insurance plan will pay the medically necessary bill. The insurance plan will pay as if you stayed within the network for treatment. Your co-pays will apply.

How big is a network? That depends on the Medicare Advantage plan. Some networks are called HMO's, another is a PPO, and still another is called PFFS.

Health Maintenance Organization (HMO)

HMO stands for Health Maintenance Organizations. HMO's are smaller networks. An HMO usually covers a certain area of physicians, hospitals and outpatient facilities where the beneficiary lives. If you live in Tampa, Florida, you live in Hillsborough County. Some Medicare Advantage plans will only cover contracted physicians, hospitals and outpatient facilities within Hillsborough County.

If you sought treatment with a physician in Pasco County, the physician may not be in the network, and you may be responsible for the majority or the entire bill. Other HMO plans cover larger areas within a State. It's your responsibility to determine if the area the HMO covers fits your lifestyle and needs.

Being on an HMO Medicare Advantage plan gives you limited choices for treatment. If you were diagnosed with lung cancer, you would have to be treated by Oncologists in your network. If you wanted to get a second opinion from Sloan Kettering Hospital in New York, you would be *denied!* (I'm not a fan of anything I'm limited to.)

You must understand you are not free to choose any doctor or hospital on an HMO. The benefit of not paying a monthly premium or a deductible has its consequences. Be prepared for them! You must do your research on HMO Medicare Advantage plans before you enroll.

Preferred Physician Organization (PPO)

Another type of Medicare Advantage network is the PPO which stands for Preferred Physician Organization. The PPO is larger than a traditional HMO. Some Medicare Advantage PPO plans are established by regions. Meaning, if you lived in Clearwater, FL, you could see all the physicians, hospitals and outpatient facilities contracted with the PPO Medicare Advantage plan in Florida *only*. If you wanted a second opinion at MD Anderson Cancer Center in Texas, you would be denied! You would be restricted under the PPO plan to seek treatment in Florida.

Due to more choices in physicians, hospitals and outpatient facilities, you will pay *higher* co-pays for being on a PPO plan. How much higher? Let's say you were admitted into the hospital for five days into a network hospital. On an HMO plan, you might pay a co-pay of $875 for a five day stay as a hospital inpatient. On a PPO, your co-pay may be $1,500. This is for the same amount of time as a hospital inpatient. Again, it's your responsibility to understand the area your PPO represents and your co-pay for benefits under the PPO Medicare Advantage plan. Do your due diligence.

Private Fee-For-Service Plan (PFFS)

The third type of Medicare Advantage network is the Private Fee-For-Service Plan (PFFS). In the PFFS, the plan determines how much it will pay doctors, other health care providers, and hospitals. It is also determined how much you must pay when you get care.

If you join a PFFS Plan that has a network, you can see any of the network physicians who have agreed to treat plan members. You can also choose an out-of-network doctor, hospital, or other provider, who accepts the plan's terms, but you may pay more.

You can go to any Medicare-approved physician, hospital or outpatient facility that accepts the plan's payment terms and *agrees* to treat you. Not all providers will.

You must determine costs prior to your visit. Many physicians need to be contacted prior to making appointments. The physician must agree to the payment terms of the PFFS plan before you are treated. This must be done prior to *each* visit. For each service you receive, make sure your doctors, hospitals, and outpatient facilities agree to treat you under the plan and accept the plan's payment terms.

Out-of-network doctors, hospitals, and other outpatient facilities may decide not to treat you even if they have seen you before.

You must be diligent in understanding the terms of a PFFS plan. You may have more choices of physicians, hospitals and outpatient facilities. You may also have to pay higher out-of-pocket co-pays. Organizational skills are essential to be on this type of Medicare Advantage plan. If you're good at planning your health care with physicians and outpatient facilities, this could be the plan for you.

Special Needs Plan (SNPs)

Another type of Medicare Advantage plan is the Special Needs Plan (SNPs) which limits membership to people with specific diseases or characteristics. People diagnosed with diabetes who take insulin, people with chronic obstructive pulmonary disease (COPD), and people diagnosed with cardiovascular disease are examples of people enrolled in Special Needs Plans. Special Needs Plans tailor their benefits, physician choices, and drug formularies to best meet the specific needs of the groups they serve.

Generally, you must get your care and services from physicians, hospitals or an outpatient facility in the Medicare Special Needs Plan network. (Except in an emergency or need urgent care, such as care you get for a sudden illness or injury that needs medical care right away).

If you have End Stage Renal Disease (ESRD) you will be able to receive dialysis while away and out of network.

Medicare SNPs typically have specialists in the diseases or conditions that affect their members.

You can read about Special Needs Plans on my website: www.callsamm.com

Or contact a SAMM Medicare Adviser if you need more information on Special Needs Plans.

CHAPTER 4
Special Election Periods (SEP)

Special Election Periods

The annual enrollment period is the period of time when you can change your Medicare Advantage Plan. Each year, beginning on October 15 and ending December 7 (Pearl Harbor Day) at 11:59 PM, you can enroll in a different plan if you choose to do so.

If you like the Medicare plan you're currently on, you don't have to do anything. Your coverage will continue without you having to do anything. If you decide to change your Medicare Advantage plan, the changes will take effect on January 1st of the new year.

Is this the only time you can change your Medicare Advantage plan?

Yes, unless you have a special circumstance that is recognized by Medicare. These special circumstances would allow you to change your Medicare plan under what's called a *Special Election Period*.

Special circumstances remind me of an incident I experienced with one of my clients. She had a special circumstance that she wasn't even aware of. Here's her story.

My friend, Connie, asked me to talk to her mother, Bea. (Yes, this is the same Bea who referred me to Janet in the previous account.) Connie said her mom keeps receiving letters from the state telling her she is eligible for food stamps. The problem is Bea is adamant that she does not want to be on food stamps. I told Connie I'd be happy to talk with Bea.

When I arrived at Bea's house she invited me in to sit at the kitchen table and have a glass of ice tea with her. I accepted the invitation and pulled out my pen and paper to scribble notes as we chatted.

In our conversation I learned that Bea had been widowed at a young age and worked hard to raise her children on her own and to keep the bills paid.

"I never took any handouts," Bea said proudly. "When you need something, you just do what you have to do. I didn't take any handouts then and I'm certainly not taking any handouts now."

After reviewing Bea's income and assets, I could see she would most likely qualify for assistance from the state. Bea could apply for food stamps, the Medicare Savings Program (which pays her Medicare Part B premium), and Extra Help with her prescription drug coverage.

When I explained what assistance was available, Bea nearly hit the roof. "I told you I don't want any handouts. I can pay my own way," she stated in no uncertain terms.

"Bea, I hear you loud and clear," I told her. "I'm here to explain everything you're entitled to. If you decide you don't want to apply for those services, we won't apply. The point here is that you paid taxes all those years that you worked. You paid extra taxes specifically for your Medicare, so you could utilize those services today."

Now I had her attention.

"I personally feel you should let the government take the money out of the Medicare fund for you. After all, you already put the money into it."

Bea thought for a minute, then said, "You have a point. But that doesn't mean I have to take food stamps."

"You're right. You don't have to accept food stamps. If you feel you have enough money coming in to pay for groceries, *and* your medicine *and* your bills, then you don't have to apply for food stamps."

Bea stood up and stepped over to the fridge to get us more tea. I could tell she was thinking over what she was hearing.

"I had no idea there were so many programs available," she said. "I thought the only assistance available was welfare and food stamps."

Then she said, "Okay. Let's apply for the Part B Premium and forget the food stamps." Bea had made her decision.

"If your application is accepted," I explained, "you need to know you'll most likely receive the prescription drug assistance. It goes hand in hand with the Medicare Savings Program you'd be accepted into,"

"I'm good with that."

"And by applying for the Medicare Savings Program," I continued, "you'll save a little over one hundred dollars in your social security check. You will also pay little or no co-pays on your Medicare Advantage Plan. The Extra Help will make your co-pays for prescription drugs very affordable.

"Each year, the state will ask you to complete a review to see if you still qualify. I can help you fill out the review each year if you'd like."

"Yes, I'd appreciate that very much. I feel much better now, Diane. Thank you for listening to me and helping me understand everything." Then she added, "You're my Earth angel!"

"Thanks for that kind compliment," I said. "It's made me happy that I could help you. Every time I help someone with their Medicare, I feel like I'm paying back my grandparents for everything they did for me growing up."

Bea had an income that allowed her to apply for state assistance. Being accepted into the Medicare Savings Program is going to allow Bea to save over $1,200 through the next year. Don't you think that means the world to someone who makes less than $950 a month?

The special circumstance triggers a special election period for Bea. After receiving her acceptance letter from the state regarding the Medicare Savings Program, I enrolled Bea in a Medicare/Medicaid plan (aka Medi-Medi) that would begin the first day of the next month.

Bea is now on the Medicare Plan that fit her best. My mission had been accomplished.

Our example with Bea shows one special circumstance; now let's take a look at other special circumstances.

Move to a New Address

1. If you move to a new address and the location is out of your Medicare Advantage Plan's service area.

   Some Medicare Plans have limited networks of physicians and facilities. A different town may not have contracted doctors or facilities in your plan.
2. You may move to a new address that is in your plan's service area, but you may have new plan options in your new area.

   Your new town or county may have plan options that you weren't aware of before. Take advantage of researching Medicare Advantage Plans in your new town or county.
3. You moved back to the United States after living in a different country.

   That one is pretty self-explanatory.
4. You may have just moved into, currently live in, or you are moving out of a skilled nursing facility (SNF), or long-term care hospital.

   Remember, a SNF is a nursing facility with the staff and equipment to give skilled nursing care. Because of that you're entitled to switch to a different Medicare Advantage plan or go back on Original Medicare. You may add a Medi-Gap plan and a stand-alone prescription drug plan at that time also. You can make these changes while you are still living in a SNF or you have two months after you move out of the SNF to make changes.
5. You may have been just released from jail.

   You have two months from the month you are released to enroll in a Medicare Advantage plan. You can make changes to or join a Prescription Drug plan if you needed to.

Your coverage is ending from your Employer, Union, or Cobra.

You have a total of eight months from the month you lose your coverage to enroll in a Medicare Plan.

You're Eligible to Receive Medicare and Medicaid.

You're considered dual eligible. Your income and assets may allow you to receive assistance from the state in which you reside, just as my client, Bea, did. Search your state name + Medicaid to find out if you qualify to apply for state assistance.

You can join a Medicare Advantage Plan, switch to a different one or drop your Medicare Advantage Plan and go back on Original Medicare whenever you want. Your new plan will start the first day of the following month.

These are the most common special circumstances where you will have a special election period to join or change your Medicare Plan. To view more special circumstances that would allow a special election period, go to www.medicare.gov and click on the tab, *When can I join a health or drug plan?* Then click on *Special Circumstances*. You can also go to my website, www.callsamm.com and click on the SEP tab.

If you have a special circumstance that creates a special election period and you change your Medicare Advantage Plan, your signature on the new application will apprise Medicare of the change. You will not have to contact Medicare to advise them you are changing plans. If you are changing from a Medicare Supplement Insurance Plan to a Medicare Advantage Plan, you will need to contact the Supplement Insurance Company to advise them you are cancelling the Supplement Insurance Plan and enrolling in a Medicare Advantage Plan.

CHAPTER 5

Turning 65

You're turning 65 this year! If you've worked for ten consecutive years, or worked forty quarters prior to turning 65, and you paid into payroll taxes, you're eligible for Medicare.

How Do You Enroll In Medicare?

If you are not receiving Social Security benefits (i.e., still working) during the three months prior to your 65th birthday, you should contact Social Security to enroll in Medicare.

You can enroll online at http://www.socialsecurity.gov/medicare/apply.html. You can call Social Security at 800-633-4227. Or you can look up your local Social Security office by visiting https://secure.ssa.gov/ICON/main.jsp

If you're already receiving social security benefits you should receive your red, white and blue Medicare card in the mail. If you don't receive your Medicare ID card in the mail the first day of the month prior to your 65th birthday, visit your local social security office to find out what the delay is.

How Long is the Open Enrollment Period?

The year you turn 65, you can sign up during the seven-month period that begins three months before the month you turn 65 (this includes the month you turn 65), and ends three months after the month you turn 65.

Example:

Bill turns 65 in July and it's currently February. Bill can enroll three months prior to his 65th birthday, which would be April, May or June. If Bill enrolls in Medicare during April, May or June, his Medicare will be effective July 1st (the month of his 65th birthday).

If Bill enrolls in July, his Medicare effective date will be in August.

If Bill waits until August, his effective date will be in October.

If he waits until September, his Medicare effective date won't be until November.

If Bill waits until October to enroll, his Medicare effective date won't be until January.

Bill won't be assessed any penalties for enrolling in August, September or October, but he delays his enrollment in Medicare each month he waits.

If Bill enrolls in Medicare past October, his effective date will be between January and March of the following year. Bill will also be assessed a late penalty, which is 10% for each twelve months he didn't enroll in Medicare during his initial enrollment period.

This is why I always tell my clients that it's always better to enroll early than late.

Medicare Supplement Enrollment

If you're turning 65 and you decide you'd like to enroll in a *Medicare Supplement* plan, you can enroll *six months* prior to your 65th birthday. The Medicare Supplement policy will not take effect until the first day of the month you turn 65, but you'll have peace of mind knowing you had enough time to research the different types of Medicare plans and choose to enroll in the plan that fit you best.

In this case, Bill could enroll in a Medicare Supplement plan as early as January. Bill's 65th birthday is in July and he can enroll in the Medicare Supplement plan six months prior to his 65th birthday, which would be January. The Medicare Supplement plan will be effective July 1, the month he turns 65.

If you're still working and on your employer's health insurance plan, you may delay enrollment into Medicare Part B. You'll not be penalized while you're on continuous group health insurance coverage. When your employer's policy terminates, or when you retire, you may then enroll in Medicare Part B most likely with the same guaranteed issue you would have been entitled to when you were 65.

If you've paid into payroll taxes for ten years, or worked forty quarters while paying payroll taxes, you're entitled to Medicare Part A, with no premium. You should enroll in Medicare Part A when you are turning 65, whether you're still working or not. You'll enjoy the added hospital insurance alongside your employer's policy. With extra coverage and no added premium, why wouldn't you enroll in Medicare Part A while still working?

Here's a story about one of my clients who followed my advice.

Carl owned a small car repair shop. Carl was turning 67 and was ready to retire. He had spoken to me three years earlier when he was 64. At that time, he was under an employee-sponsored health insurance plan for himself and his employees.

Carl wasn't sure if he should be on Medicare or not when he turned 65. After discussing his finances and his health insurance needs, I advised him to enroll in Medicare Part A, but to hold off on enrolling in Medicare Part B until he was ready to retire from the repair shop.

Carl did just that. One year later, he was hospitalized for four days. With the coverage from his health insurance plan and Medicare Part A, Carl didn't have any out-of-pocket expenses. Carl can now enroll in Part B without having any late penalty, because he had continuous health coverage.

Carl had contacted me early enough to look at all his options. With the proper knowledge, he decided with confidence to enroll in Medicare Part A and to defer his Part B enrollment while on his employer health coverage. Carl saved an estimated $2,500 in out-of-pocket expenses by deferring his Part B enrollment.

Everyone has unique life situations. It's important to review your options with a Medicare Adviser prior to enrolling in Medicare.

CHAPTER 6

End Stage Renal Disease (ESRD)

Medicare defines End Stage Renal Disease, (ESRD) as permanent kidney failure that requires a regular course of dialysis or a kidney transplant.

Anyone, at any age, can have kidney failure. A person with ESRD is entitled to Medicare Part A and may enroll in Medicare Part B if they are diagnosed with ESRD. If a person is on individual health insurance, or has no health insurance, a qualified Medicare recipient will begin Medicare benefits four months after dialysis begins. You would still wait four months if you are working and on an employer sponsored insurance plan. The difference is your employer plan would most likely pay the majority of the ESRD treatment costs.

You can apply for Original Medicare as soon as you are diagnosed with ESRD. You should contact social security by phone, in person, or apply for Medicare online at www.ssa.gov

Original Medicare Part A will cover 80% of the Medicare allowable cost of dialysis you receive as a hospital inpatient. You would owe the remaining 20%.

Your Medicare Part B would cover 80% of the Medicare allowable cost of dialysis you receive at a Medicare Approved Dialysis outpatient center. You would owe the remaining 20% of the Medicare Allowable charge.

I have found that the biggest problem my clients face is being able to pay the remaining 20% of the bill. Receiving dialysis three times a week for a month is extremely expensive. A local dialysis center here in Tampa, Florida, charges roughly $23,000.00 for dialysis treatments three times a week for one month. Who has $4,600 a month (your 20% co-insurance) sitting around to pay for dialysis?

That's why educating people about Medicare is so important! You need to know these answers before you have a serious illness or injury.

Let's look at a possible solution.

If you enrolled in Original Medicare (Part A & Part B) when you were turning 65 and purchased a type F Supplement Insurance Policy to go with it, you would now be charged for the remaining 20% of the Medicare allowable bill. You would pay a monthly premium for the Medicare Supplement insurance for the rest of your life. Currently, by paying that premium, you would not have to stick your hand in your pocket again for medical expenses. (That applies to medical expenses, not drugs).

Nada! Zilch! Zero! That's what's known as peace of mind, folks.

There are other types of Medicare Supplement insurance policies that would cover most, if not all, of the 20% responsibility of your Medicare allowable bill. Contact your Medicare Insurance Agent or log on to http://www.medicare.gov/supplement-other-insurance/index.html to research more information regarding Medicare Supplement policies. You can also go to my website at www.callsamm.com and click on the tab, Medicare Supplement Policies.

Medicare Part A and/or Part B will pay 80% of your dialysis bill. You have the dialysis center directly bill your Medicare Supplement insurance for the remaining 20% of the Medicare allowable charges. That's it! No co-pays, no deductibles, no fees.

Medicare Advantage Plans

Another possible solution is looking at Medicare Advantage Plans. A few Medicare Advantage Plans will cover the 20% out-of-pocket expense you would owe for kidney dialysis if the dialysis is performed at a Medicare-certified dialysis facility which provides outpatient maintenance dialysis treatments. The Medicare Advantage Plan would *not* cover the 20% out-of-pocket expense, if you had the dialysis treatment at an outpatient hospital facility. In other words, you couldn't schedule dialysis treatments as an outpatient in a hospital, if you wanted the Medicare Advantage plan to pay the 20% co-pay.

If you are already diagnosed with ESRD, you will not be able to change from your existing plan to a new plan. The *only time* you'll be granted a special election period for having ESRD is if Medicare terminates its contract with a Medicare Advantage Insurance company.

Forced Special Election Period

At the time of this writing, many of my clients had experienced a special election period when *Physician United Plan* (PUP), was forced to liquidate by a Florida judge.

PUP is a Medicare Advantage Plan that was contracted with Medicare. PUP provided an HMO network in Florida. On June 9, 2014, Charles Francis, a Florida Circuit Court judge, ordered Physicians United Plan, Inc. into receivership under the Florida Department of Financial Services (DFS), which liquidated effective July 1, 2014. This, in turn, terminated PUP's contract with Medicare, leaving about 40,000 Medicare Beneficiaries without a Medicare Advantage Plan.

Florida's Department of Financial Services reviewed the court's decision and issued a special election plan for the PUP beneficiaries, and moved all PUP beneficiaries back onto Original Medicare.

They also randomly issued Part D Prescription Drug Plans to each of the PUP beneficiaries due to the fact Part A and Part B of Original Medicare do not provide common prescription drug coverage in their benefits. The Part D Plans were made retroactive to June 1, 2014. All the PUP beneficiaries were utilizing their Original Medicare Part A & Part B benefits as their only health plan.

The Medicare Prescription Drug Plan Providers began sending out bills to the PUP beneficiaries for $21.00. While these Medicare beneficiaries were on a PUP plan, they did not have a premium for their prescription drug coverage. The $21.00 bill was a premium for being randomly assigned coverage to a Part D Prescription Drug Plan for the month of June, 2014.

The special election period granted to PUP beneficiaries was effective from June, 2014 through August 31, 2014. During this special election period, Medicare beneficiaries who were previously on a PUP plan would be granted the opportunity to go on a different Medicare Advantage Plan or a Medi-Gap plan during this time period. If the Medicare beneficiary chose not to enroll in a different Medicare Plan, they would remain with Original Medicare as their health plan and they would have the option to add a stand-alone Prescription Drug Plan which would include a monthly premium.

If you recall, Original Medicare provides a large network of physicians and facilities across America. Medicare pays 80% of the Medicare approved bill and you owe the remaining 20%. You have a Part A deductible of $1,260.00 when you are admitted to the hospital. You will pay the $1,260.00 deductible *each* time you are admitted to the hospital for a new illness or injury *or* you are admitted to the hospital for the *same* illness or injury after 60 consecutive days.

For all your other outpatient medical services, doctor appointments, blood work, x-rays etc. you have an annual deductible of $147.00, then you pay 20% of the Medicare approved bill.

That can be a very expensive health care plan for most Medicare beneficiaries. Persons who received assistance from the State of Florida as Qualified Medicare Beneficiaries (QMB) could continue to be on Original Medicare, if they chose to do so. The State of Florida would assist qualified Medicare beneficiaries with paying the premium for Part B of Medicare (currently $104.90) and paying for deductibles, co-insurance and co-pays under Part A, Part B and Part D of Medicare. Other individuals qualified for limited State benefits, due to their income.

Some of my clients who were on a PUP plan were also diagnosed with ESRD.

A client named John telephoned me asking for advice. They were on the PUP (Physician United Plan) Medicare Advantage Plan and both had lost their Medicare Advantage coverage. John was very concerned for his wife Jackie who suffered with ESRD.

Jackie was currently in dialysis treatments and he was worried as to how Jackie would get on a new Medicare Advantage Plan. I set an appointment to meet with this couple.

Sitting at their kitchen table, John began to tell me his situation with his PUP Medicare plan.

He said, "We don't have one. That's what is happening."

I could instantly see the confusion. "You are both currently under Original Medicare. You didn't lose your benefits under Original Medicare, just the benefits under the PUP Medicare Advantage plan."

"What does that mean?" Jackie wanted to know. I could see the fear on her face.

"You still have your red, white and blue card from Medicare, correct?"

They both said yes they had those cards.

"When you enrolled in Medicare, you enrolled in Part A and Part B," I explained. "You're still enrolled in the government program. That has not ended. When you enrolled in the PUP Medicare Advantage plan, you allowed PUP to manage your Medicare plan, with co-pays and a network of doctors and facilities. You still had the same benefits under Part A and Part B of Original Medicare. It was how you made payments for treatment and hospitalization that would be different."

Then I asked Jackie, "When you saw your Nephrologist, what did you pay for a co-pay?"

"I think it was $5.00," she replied.

"Correct. Under the PUP Medicare Advantage Plan, you have co-pays. I call it the pay as you go plan. You have a co-pay each time you see a specialist. That co-pay for your PUP plan to see the specialist is $5.00.

"Now, how much is your co-pay for your dialysis treatment?"

It was John who answered. "Our co-pay is 20% of the Medicare paid amount."

"That's correct," I said. "Under PUP's Medicare Advantage plan, the plan charges you the same amount as Original Medicare does for dialysis treatment, which is 20% of the Medicare charged amount. If Medicare states it will pay $1000.00 per dialysis treatment, then they will pay $800.00, which is 80%. The remaining 20% or $200.00 would be your responsibility."

Next I needed to know about Jackie's treatment schedule which I learned was three days a week. Her next appointment was scheduled for the following day. So I told her, "When you go to the facility, show the receptionist your red, white and blue card. Advise them you are now on Original Medicare. Keep all your scheduled appointments. The only thing that's changed is who is being billed for the services. Currently, that would be Original Medicare. Your plan is now with Original Medicare."

When I left their home, I knew I had my work cut out for me. I needed to find the best solution to Jackie's problem. What plan was best for Jackie? Original Medicare? Or another Medicare Advantage plan?

During my assessment, I had determined that a Medi-Gap plan was not an option. Jackie and John could not afford the monthly premiums for a Medi-Gap plan and still run their household. I would need to find an option that fit Jackie's unique situation.

After my research, I selected one Medicare Advantage plan from Company C that would suit Jackie best. Jackie had certain doctors she wanted to retain. She was taking costly medications and also had other medical issues to deal with.

After paying their monthly bills, this couple didn't have much money left. Company C's Medicare Advantage plan fit those needs with one *very important* benefit! The co-pay for kidney dialysis treatments at a private, free-standing unit would cost them $0.00. That's right, nada.

Another important benefit of the Medicare Advantage plan from Company C was that the maximum out-of-pocket expenses Jackie would pay in one calendar year was $3,400.00. If Jackie ever paid $3,400.00 out of her pocket for medical care during the year, the Company C Medicare Advantage plan would pay for all the remaining medically needed care for the rest of the calendar year that Medicare would pay for.

I couldn't wait to discuss this option with John and Jackie.

At our next meeting, John and Jackie both agreed that the Company C Medicare Advantage plan would be best for Jackie. John decided to enroll in the same plan, due to the benefits of the plan.

The Medicare Survival Guide

Jackie informed me that she had had no trouble at the dialysis center. They took her Medicare card and billed Medicare for payment.

The effective date for the Company C Medicare Advantage plan was July 1. I advised Jackie that she would be responsible for 20% of the Medicare charged cost for the remaining dialysis treatments for the month of June. When the Company C Medicare Advantage plan took effect July 1, she would no longer be responsible for that 20% charge for dialysis treatments, as long as she continued to go to the free-standing dialysis center.

John and Jackie were ecstatic. They couldn't believe how much money they were going to save by being on the Company "C" Medicare Advantage plan.

"It's fantastic," Jackie said. "Thank you so much for helping us find the right Medicare plan,"

"How are you in regards to medications for the rest of the month?" I asked.

Jackie said, "Great. I don't need any more prescriptions until July. I do receive drugs at the dialysis center in my IV though."

"Are the drugs you receive in your IV directly related to your dialysis treatment?"

"Yes," Jackie replied. "They are for anemia."

I told her that the drugs she received in her IV at the dialysis center were most likely covered under her Part B insurance. I suggested that she ask the nurse at the dialysis center at her next visit.

"The drugs you are receiving are included in the Company C Medicare Advantage plan formulary," I explained. "If you have questions about the coverage of a Part B drug, look in the plan's formulary or call the plan's customer service number located on the back of your plan's ID card."

Surprise Call

Two weeks later, I received a voice mail from John telling me that Jackie had been denied coverage in the Company C Medicare plan due to the fact she currently had ESRD.

I had John read the letter to me over the phone. As he had stated, the letter indicated since Jackie currently had ESRD, she was not qualified to enroll in their Medicare Advantage Plan program. The letter also said that Jackie would need to remain on Original Medicare and she would need to enroll in a stand-alone prescription drug plan.

In no uncertain terms, I told John that Company C was wrong. PERIOD.

When Medicare takes a specific action against a Medicare Advantage Plan, (such as terminating the plan), and it affects its beneficiaries, a special election period is determined on a case-by-case basis.

In the case against PUP, a special election period was determined by the Center for Medicare & Medicaid Services, which allowed PUP beneficiaries to change to another type of Medicare Plan until August 31, 2014. If a PUP beneficiary decided *not* to enroll in another type of Medicare Plan, they would remain on Original Medicare.

This special election period was granted to all PUP beneficiaries. Even to beneficiaries with ESRD. There is a one-time exception for beneficiaries with ESRD to change Medicare plans, and this is it!

I asked Jackie if she wanted me to call Company C and we would have a 3-way conversation. She agreed.

We got on the line and spoke to a customer representative. After Jackie introduced herself and gave the rep her identifying information, she told them about the coverage denial. The rep confirmed the denial and told Jackie she was currently enrolled in Original Medicare and would have no problem receiving future dialysis treatments. Jackie asked me to come on the line and explain to the rep about the special election period.

I did just that, explaining about the special election period for Jackie and stated she should be entitled to enroll in their Medicare Advantage Plan. The rep was still adamant so I asked to speak with a supervisor.

After a long wait, a supervisor came on the line.

Again I explained the situation, this time to a supervisor; and I again requested they allow Jackie to enroll in their Medicare Advantage Plan due to the SEP.

At that point the supervisor asked to speak to Jackie. She was already exhausted from that day's dialysis treatment, but she spoke to the supervisor and again asked to be enrolled in their Medicare Advantage Plan.

Finally, John's patience was beginning to wear thin. He took the phone from Jackie and told the supervisor that if they didn't comply with his wife's request, he would have to make a formal complaint with Medicare.

I once again reiterated the language from the Medicare regulations, and the supervisor stated she would look into it and be back on the line in a few minutes.

I was thinking, *What the heck is going on? I'm on the phone with Company C's enrollment supervisor, who doesn't know the regulations regarding ESRD enrollments?*

[What would some other beneficiary have done if faced with this situation and no one was there to help? I think you can guess. They would have caved in. "Oh. Okay then. I'll just use my red, white and blue Medicare ID card. And I'll pay 20% of the Medicare bill and go bankrupt. Thank you so much for your help. And have a great day!"]

The Company C supervisor came back on the line after what seemed like an eternity. She began to apologize for the letter and told John that Jackie would be enrolled in their Medicare Advantage Plan and that the effective date would be made retroactive to July 1.

The supervisor told me I was 100% correct and they thought that Jackie was only trying to switch Medicare Advantage Plans.

The supervisor didn't seem to realize the PUP plan had been terminated by Medicare.

Really? I had said it two times. Jackie had said it two times. And then the supervisor also referred to the PUP plan being terminated a couple of times.

All right – so the supervisor was trying to save face. I get it. The point was, now Jackie is enrolled in Company C's Medicare Advantage Plan and will not have to pay *any* out-of-pocket co-pays for the dialysis treatment.

Now this couple has a plan that fits them like a glove.

You should have a Medicare Advisor that you can call to discuss Medicare issues with. Your Medicare Advisor should be extremely knowledgeable in Medicare and willing to take your calls. That person should be willing and able to help you in situations where you can't rectify an issue. Don't be afraid to tell your agent that you need them to help you with an issue you can't fix. If they tell you they can't do it and to call customer service – it's time to find someone else.

In today's world, you need a Medicare Adviser you can trust. A Medicare Adviser you can count on when you need help. Someone who has the answer or knows how to find it.

Don't settle for mediocrity. You deserve excellence.

Dialysis Medications

For dialysis medications, Medicare Part A pays a portion if you are receiving treatment in the hospital as an inpatient. Medicare Part B pays a portion if you are receiving treatment at a Medicare approved dialysis center as an outpatient. This time, you will pay 100% of the bill if you don't purchase a stand-alone prescription drug plan while on Original Medicare. To offset the costs, you purchase a drug plan that includes a formulary (a book that lists drugs accepted on the insurance) and pay a small monthly premium. You will also have co-pays according to the drug plan's formulary. They divide drugs into tiers. Each drug in the formulary is assigned to a tier that has specific co-pay assigned for that tier.

If you're taking the brand drug *Zofran* (for nausea), you would look it up in your plan's formulary. You find *Zofran* and see it is assigned as a tier 5 (specialty drug). You turn to your prescription plan's tier 5 information and you see you will pay around $24.00 for a 30 day supply of *Zofran*.

That's how you determine the cost for your prescribed medication. To find the stand-alone drug plan that will fit you best, go to www.medicare.gov and research the information on Part D drug plans.

If you're under the age of 65, Medicare will continue to assist in paying for medically needed treatment twelve months after you stop dialysis treatment.

If you receive a kidney transplant, Medicare will continue to assist in paying for medically needed treatment for three years after you receive the transplant.

It is important to do due diligence when looking for the type of Medicare Plan which will give you the best options in case of a serious illness or injury. You may conduct research on the medicare.gov website or review information on my website www.callsamm.com for more information regarding ESRD.

CHAPTER 7
Veterans

I love veterans. I've been around military men and women my whole life. I respect the fact that they fought for my freedom. Freedom means I can practice any religion I choose, carry a gun to protect myself and my property, and to love and admire the New York Yankees.

In my opinion, veterans don't receive what they deserve when they come home. If I was President of the United States, I would ensure that every man and woman who served in a conflict or war for the United States, would never have to worry about health insurance for the rest of their life. I would also ensure they had a pension. If they stood on any soil to protect the rights of any US citizen, and they had to come home the same day due to being shot in the buttocks, they would receive some form of a pension.

Obviously, I'm not the President so I'll just advise you of the facts involving Medicare for veterans.

In chapter 1, we talked about who was eligible for Medicare. One of the criteria was if a person was receiving Supplemental Security Income (SSI) for a disability, the individual would be eligible for Medicare in 24 months after receiving their first SSI payment. Veterans fit into that category. When a veteran is receiving SSI for a disability, he or she is eligible for Medicare after 24months.

Veterans who are career vets (serving 20-plus years of service) will receive a pension and Tricare as their health insurance. When they turn 65, they will also receive original Medicare Part A & Part B. A winning combination.

Veterans receive their care at Veteran Administration facilities across the US. As long as they see a physician in a VA facility, they will be able to utilize their veteran benefits.

What happens if the veteran is eligible for Medicare on top of his or her veteran benefits? They should enroll in Medicare. A veteran who wants to be seen only at a veteran administrative facility will fare well if enrolling in Medicare Part A.

Remember, Part A is for inpatient hospital services, Skilled Nursing Facility services, and Hospice Care. If a veteran was driving to a veteran administration facility and got into an accident while driving there, the veteran would be taken to the local emergency room if treatment was required.

If the veteran only has veteran benefits for treatment at a veteran administrative facility and the treatment needed is not life threatening, the veteran may be responsible for the majority of the hospital bill.

If the veteran was enrolled in Medicare Part A and was taken to the hospital and had to be admitted for a broken leg and broken ribs, Medicare Part A would most likely pick up any remaining balance of the hospital bill the veterans administration did not cover.

What about Medicare Part B? Remember Medicare Part B covers outpatient services. Let's look at one of my client's story as a good example.

I met Danny while visiting one of my clients in an apartment complex. Danny was driving in his motorized scooter while I was taking my briefcase and supplies out of my car. Danny asked who I was there to see.

"A woman in building 103," I told him.

He pulled to a stop by the rear of my car and said, "I know everyone in building 103. Good people."

"That's great news," I replied as I closed my trunk lid.

"You a lawyer?" Danny asked.

"No, I'm not a lawyer," I answered with a chuckle. "I'm a Medicare Adviser. I'm here to review a Medicare plan to see if any changes are necessary."

Danny smiled and said, "Cool. Can I get Medicare?"

"It depends." I replied. I went down the list of a few of requirements for being eligible. When I was reciting benefits related to those who receive disability benefits, Danny's face lit up like a Christmas tree.

"I'm disabled," he said. "And I'm a veteran too. Does that count?"

"What branch of the military were you in, Danny?"

"Army."

"Thank you very much for your service," I said. "I appreciate you putting your life on the line for the freedom of all of us at home. I really do."

Then I told him that I wouldn't be able to answer his questions just then because of my current appointment. He then asked me for my phone number and I handed him one of my business cards.

"If you'd like to discuss things another time, call me."

As I climbed the stairs to Cheryl's apartment, Danny said, "I'll call you tomorrow." And with that he drove away in his scooter.

And he did just that. Danny called me as he had stated he would. I scheduled an appointment with Danny at his apartment.

"Thanks for coming," Danny said as he opened his door and invited me in.

Danny lived in an efficiency apartment. The bedroom and living room were all in one room. A small kitchen was attached and a small bathroom on the opposite side. There was a metal folding chair in the middle of the room with a tray table opened up in front of it.

"Have a seat over there," he said motioning me to the chair. "I'll sit next to you in my scooter."

Because he was such an easy person to talk to, we talked for well over an hour. I was saddened to hear about his injuries from the Iraqi War. Danny loved the Army and was upset that he couldn't stay in. He'd been sent home to recover from a permanent disability.

Danny was already enrolled in Medicare, but he had no idea that he was. No one had explained to him or told him what his benefits were. He received all his treatment at the veterans' hospital. He didn't drive, but took the city bus to the veterans' hospital.

Then I asked him where he'd go if he were hit by a car while driving his scooter?

"I guess I'd have to go the emergency room."

"That's right. You'd be taken to the nearest emergency room. That's policy for emergency responders. And if you were taken to the emergency room for treatment, and had to be admitted into the hospital for a week, who would pay your medical bill?"

Danny thought about that for a minute. "I guess the veteran's hospital. Right?"

I could tell he didn't really know.

"If you were admitted into a non-government hospital for medically necessary treatment, the veteran hospital benefits would most likely pay for the majority of the bill, but not all of it. As soon as you were stable enough, you'd be transferred to the veterans' hospital in order for your veteran benefits to continue."

"What if I didn't want to be transferred? Maybe I liked how the people were treating me at the hospital better."

"If you wanted to be covered by your veteran benefits, you would have to be transferred. If you wanted to remain in the non-government hospital, Medicare would pay for your Part A expenses.

"By utilizing your Medicare Part A *and* Part B benefits, you'll have additional coverage available to you. You could continue to see your doctors at the VA hospital whenever you wanted. Your veteran's benefits would continue to pay for those services.

"If something were to happen to you and you couldn't get to the VA hospital, you could be seen by a doctor who accepts Medicare or any non-government hospital and Medicare would pay for those medically needed services."

I could tell I had Danny's attention now. "You're telling me if I'm on Medicare, I can go to the VA hospital to see my doctor, or to any doctor who accepts Medicare? I have a choice?"

"Yes," I told him, "you do have a choice. If you needed prescription drugs, you'd continue to receive them at the VA hospital. If you wanted to get prescription drugs at a local pharmacy, you could purchase a stand-alone prescription drug plan. That would involve paying a monthly premium of about ten to twenty dollars a month. You would also pay co-pays for each prescription drug you bought."

"I wouldn't want to do that. I don't make too much money," Danny said. "If I wanted to just go to the VA hospital for all my medical treatment and my prescription drugs, is there any other way I could benefit from being on Medicare?"

"There certainly is. You do have other options. Let's take a look at those too."

I was going to inform Danny about Medicare Advantage Plans – the Part C of Medicare. Under law, I conducted all the proper and necessary paperwork and visual information I needed to show him, before we could begin discussing Medicare Advantage.

With that completed, I outlined different options that were available to him. Remember, Medicare Advantage Plans have networks. You must see one of the doctors in the network in order for the Medicare Advantage Plan to pay the bill. Currently, some of the Medicare Advantage Plans were offering a rebate on their Medicare Advantage Plan. Danny was keen on that type of Medicare Advantage Plan.

A rebate plan is when the Insurance Company will rebate all or some of the Medicare Part B premium each month to you, in order to get your business.

The downside is the co-pays for treatment are considerably higher than other traditional Medicare Advantage Plans. Your out-of-pocket expenses for the year are also higher, most at $6,700.00.

Danny wasn't worried about the out-of-pocket expenses. He wasn't even concerned about the higher co-pays. "I'll be receiving treatment at the VA hospital whenever I can," he said. "I plan on using the Medicare Advantage Plan only if there is an emergency."

My advice to Danny was to stay enrolled in Original Medicare and utilize his credible veteran benefits for his prescription drug coverage.

"No," he said. "If I can have my Part B premium paid for and I don't have to buy a prescription drug plan on top of it, this is how I want to go. I want to enroll in the rebate plan."

I told him that the rebate plan he wanted to enroll in could be terminated by the insurance company the following year.

"Well, if they do, we'll just look at other options," he replied.

I enrolled Danny into the Medicare Advantage rebate plan at his request. Danny is still on that rebate plan and visits the VA hospital for all his medical care.

There are a number of lessons to be learned from Danny's story. A disabled veteran receives benefits to be treated at a VA facility. Most treatment, services, and prescriptions are covered there. Treatment at a non-government facility would be covered by the veteran's benefits if it was a life threatening event. Non-life threatening treatment would not be fully covered by veteran benefits. You would be responsible to pay for any bills that were not covered by veteran benefits. Unless you were enrolled in Medicare Part A and Part B. Then you would be covered for your medically necessary bills.

Enrolling in Medicare Part A and Part B is important additional coverage for a disabled veteran, who may require medical treatment at a non-government hospital or medical facility. Enrolling in Medicare Part A and Part B allows the disabled veteran choices in medical treatment.

Having choices in medical care is one of the best options available.

If you have the opportunity for choice in your health care options, take it.

CHAPTER 8
Medicare Transsexual Surgery

Transsexual surgery was a hot topic in 2014.

Medicare and Transsexual Surgery

On May 30 2014, a Department of Health and Human Services appeals board, reversed its decision in regards to Medicare coverage of Sex-Reassignment Surgery.

Since 1981, *The Medicare National Coverage Determination Manual* denied Medicare coverage for transsexual surgery. Section 140.3 of the manual, titled, *Transgender Surgery* currently states the following:

> *Transsexual surgery, also known as sex reassignment surgery or intersex surgery, is the culmination of a series of procedures designed to change the anatomy of transsexuals to conform to their gender identity. Transsexuals are persons with an overwhelming desire to change anatomic sex because of their fixed conviction that they are members of the opposite sex. For the male-to-female, transsexual*

surgery entails castration, penectomy and vulva-vaginal construction. Surgery for the female-to-male transsexual consists of bilateral mammectomy, hysterectomy and salpingo-oophorectomy which may be followed by phalloplasty and the insertion of testicular prostheses. Transsexual surgery for sex reassignment of transsexuals is controversial. Because of the lack of well controlled, long term studies of the safety and effectiveness of the surgical procedures and attendant therapies for transsexualism, the treatment is considered experimental.

Moreover, there is a high rate of serious complications for these surgical procedures. For these reasons, transsexual surgery is not covered.

The May 30, 2014 decision changed that.

Medicare is the Federal Government Health Insurance program for beneficiaries turning sixty-five, people with certain disabilities and people with End Stage Renal Disease (ESRD). Medicare previously denied Medicare coverage for sex-reassignment surgery due to the treatment being considered experimental and controversial.

Now, most medical groups, including the AMA and the APA consider the surgery to be a safe option for those suffering from gender dysphoria, a condition characterized by intense discomfort — or incongruence, with one's birth sex, according to the legal definition.

Roni Caryn Rabin, a reporter for the New York Times wrote in an article dated May 30, 2014,

> *Jennifer Levi, director of the Transgender Rights Project of <u>Gay and Lesbian Advocates and Defenders</u>, who filed the challenge on Ms. Mallon's behalf, said the board had reviewed the safety and efficacy of sex reassignment surgery,*

closely examining the <u>medical literature</u>, including studies that followed people for a decade or more after surgery.

"The decision brings federal Medicare policy up to 21st-century standards for transgender people, and acknowledges that there's no scientific or medical basis for categorically excluding coverage of sex reassignment surgery for people who need it," Ms. Levi said.

The decision comes from a lawsuit initiated by Denee Mallon, a 74 year-old army veteran from Albuquerque, New Mexico. Ms. Mallon challenged the Medicare policy after her request for sex-reassignment surgery had been denied. Miss Mallon was born male, but lives her life as a woman. With the reversal of the Medicare policy, Miss Mallon is planning on having the surgery, as stated in the article.

The decision is not to allow blanket coverage for sex-assignment surgeries. As with all Medicare procedures, a physician must request the surgery and deem it medically necessary.

The policy will review Medicare coverage for surgery only. Treatments, including hormone treatment are not included. Medicare coverage is not the same as Medicaid coverage. Medicaid is not part of the Department of Health and Human Services decision.

It appears the revised policy will allow the surgery on a case by case basis.

Hot topics can change the landscape of Medicare. I write of these topics for informational purposes only. I have no personal opinion in the matter. Transsexual surgery as a benefit of Medicare will personally affect a segment of the population. To others, it will be a conversation by the water cooler.

It is my goal to educate everyone about Medicare and changes to Medicare.

CONCLUSION

Believe it or not, there's much, much more to discuss about Medicare. However, it's my sincere hope that after reading the *Medicare Survival Guide*, you have a better understanding of at least the most important aspects of Medicare and Medicare plans.

Don't forget to visit my website, www.callsamm.com which offers a great deal of current information about Medicare for you to enjoy.

If you have any questions, don't hesitate to email me at diane@callsamm.com

Here's to another year of Medicare benefits.

Here's to helping you find the one Medicare plan that will fit you best!

REFERENCES CITED

Go to these sites for more information
1. www.medicare.gov
2. http://nyti.ms/1Euitrh Roni Caryn Rabin's NY Times Article, *"Medicare to Now Cover Sex-Change Surgery"*
3. http://go.cms.gov/1JsqKCq Invalidation of National Coverage Determination 140.3 - Transsexual Surgery
4. www.weissratings.com
5. www.standardandpoors.com
6. *http://wapo.st/1Egv0lG*
   Sarah Kliff's Washington Post Article, *"When Medicare launched, nobody had any clue whether it would work"*

ABOUT THE AUTHOR

Residing in Tampa, Florida, Diane Daniels has been involved in educating individuals about Medicare for over five years. Daniel's passion for Medicare began as a seed when she was just 10 years old. While living with her grandparents, Daniels saw firsthand how they spent so much time agonizing over medical bills while on Medicare.

Daniels was motivated to write *The Medicare Survival Guide* after realizing that with proper education, individuals could find the one Medicare plan that fit their lifestyle best. Education alleviates unexpected cost to individuals.

She has spent the last three years building her portfolio which allows her to offer over a hundred Medicare plans to prospective clients. Her long list of loyal clients speaks for itself. Owner and CEO of Senior Advocates for Medicare & Medicaid, LLC (SAMM), Daniels is a professional speaker, who gives educational Medicare presentations around the country.

SAMM trains health insurance agents to "educate – not sell."

Made in the USA
Lexington, KY
09 April 2016